ANOTHER WAY OF SEEING

essays on

TRANSFORMING LAW, POLITICS AND CULTURE

ANOTHER WAY OF SEEING

essays on

TRANSFORMING LAW, POLITICS AND CULTURE

PETER GABEL

qp

Quid Pro Books
New Orleans, Louisiana

Published in 2013 by Quid Pro Books.

ISBN 978-1-61027-198-1 (pbk.)
ISBN 978-1-61027-197-4 (hbk.)
ISBN 978-1-61027-199-8 (eBook)

qp

Quid Pro, LLC
5860 Citrus Blvd., Suite D-101
New Orleans, Louisiana 70123
www.quidprobooks.com

Publisher's Cataloging in Publication

Gabel, Peter.
　　　　Another way of seeing : essays on transforming law, politics and culture / Peter Gabel.
　　　　　　p. cm. — (Contemporary society)
　　　　Includes index.
　　　　ISBN 978-1-61027-198-1 (pbk.)
1. Political culture—United States. 2. Political psychology. 3. Law—United States—Critical legal studies. 4. Political sociology. I. Title. II. Series.
JA76.3.G42 2013　　　　　　　　　　　　　　　　　　　　　　　　306.21'762
　　　　　　　　　　　　　　　　　　　　　　　　　　　　　　　　2013936372

*To Rabbi Michael Lerner: Beloved lifelong
friend, comrade, and intellectual partner*

CONTENTS

INTRODUCTION: A SPIRITUAL-POLITICAL WAY OF SEEING   1

PART I

Law and Justice

1. IMAGINE LAW   19
2. LAW AND HIERARCHY   29
3. CRITICAL LEGAL STUDIES AS A SPIRITUAL PRACTICE   43
4. A NEW VISION OF JUSTICE: From Individual Rights to the Beloved Community   61

PART II

Politics

HISTORY, ELECTIONS, MOVEMENTS

5. WHAT IT REALLY MEANS TO SAY "LAW IS POLITICS": The Political Meaning of *Bush v. Gore*   71
6. WILL THE REAL JOHN KERRY PLEASE STAND UP   93
7. BECOMING PRESENT   95
8. OBAMA AND THE FLAG PIN   97
9. MEMO TO OBAMA: HOW TO AVOID BECOMING CO-OPTED   99
10. "YES WE CAN"?   105
11. THE SOCIAL MOVEMENT AS A PARALLEL UNIVERSE   109

PART III

Public Policy

12. Spiritualizing Foreign Policy   117
13. The Fear of Gay Marriage   131
14. A Call For Sacred Biologists   135
15. The Presence of Living Organisms   137

PART IV

Culture

16. The Spirit of Sartre   145
17. Patriotism at the Ballpark   153
18. The Portraits of Robert Bergman   161
19. Living With Illness in America   169

Afterword: The Spiritual Dimension of Social Justice   171

Permissions   185
Acknowledgments   187
Index   189
About the Author   195

ANOTHER WAY OF SEEING

essays on

TRANSFORMING LAW, POLITICS AND CULTURE

INTRODUCTION

A SPIRITUAL-POLITICAL WAY OF SEEING

THIS BOOK INCLUDES MY COLLECTED ESSAYS written roughly during the first decade of the 21st century, and is a follow-up to my prior volume *The Bank Teller and Other Essays on the Politics of Meaning* (subsequently referred to as *The Bank Teller*), which contained essays and some law review articles describing my understanding of the social meaning of historical, political, and cultural events occurring during the last part of the prior century. My aim in all this work has been to present an approach to understanding the world that shifts our emphasis on what constitutes the main shaping influence of all social reality from the material world to what might be called the spiritual dimension of social life—from the desire for things to the desire for love, community, solidarity and connection with others, or as I will explain shortly, for "mutual recognition" of our common humanity as authentic Presence.

Where we place our emphasis in interpreting the world is critical to being able to act together to influence historical events in a positive way and help to create a better world—a world more capable of realizing the yearnings of the human soul. Or in other words, our "social theory" is central to our capacity for effective and meaningful social action, in the sense that social theory is really nothing more than a way of seeing, and in order to do the right thing, to devote our energies in the time that we are here to worthwhile projects that are most likely to improve our collective lives and the world that we collectively inhabit, we must learn to see what is going on in front of us in a way that allows us to interpret its social meaning as accurately as possible.

The stakes involved in choosing between different social theories and narratives can be illustrated by a discussion of Lars von Trier's *Melancholia*—a movie that has received a great deal of attention from critics and moviegoers. In this remarkable

1

film, a woman named Justine, played by Kirsten Dunst, gets married in a wedding ceremony that is both extraordinarily opulent (vast sums of money are spent by her brother-in-law to assure that this is the happiest day of her life) and yet profoundly alienating in the sense that virtually all the characters, including Justine's parents and other family members, are represented as unhappy, selfish, and preoccupied with the details of the wedding ritual over the substance of any profound human bond.

Meanwhile, unbeknownst to most of the guests but somewhat mystically understood by Justine and less mystically and more scientifically so by her brother-in-law, a planet that has been hidden behind the sun has somehow shifted in its alignment and is rapidly heading toward earth. Although Justine is obviously deeply disturbed and disengaged while enduring the experience of her own wedding, she becomes more centered and present in the days following the wedding as the danger of collision with the errant planet—named Melancholia—becomes more likely. In the final scene, as Justine sits holding hands with her frightened sister and innocent young nephew in a hastily constructed "magic cave" that Justine has told the boy will protect them all, it is Justine who seems spiritually prepared for the apocalyptic end that awaits them and all of the world. While during the early part of the film Justine appeared to be the one doomed to disorientation and debilitating melancholia, at the end it is she who becomes at one with the profound and sudden ending of both the collective life and the collective history and culture of the human experience, of human existence itself.

The theory that has informed most of the reviews of *Melancholia* has been quite explicitly Freudian, perhaps because Freud wrote a very famous book called *Mourning and Melancholia* that addressed the way that loss—in particular unmourned loss—can create a pathological attachment to the lost object that leads one to become in-dwelling and withdrawn, to lose all interest in life, and to become quite literally vitiated of human vitality. This meaning of the word "melancholia," drawn from Freud's good work on the subject, has then been projected into the movie, so that Justine is identified as deeply "depressed" by the disturbed nature of her conditioned upbringing, which reaches a kind of apotheosis in the dysfunctional and dysphoric wedding ceremony. This depression is interpreted as a manifestation of her melancholia, her loss of vitality and interest in life. In Freud's analysis, the failure to work through the experience of loss through the process of mourning both expresses and reinforces an infantile belief on the part of the sufferer that he or she is responsible for the loss of the loved object, and this guilt not only becomes a primary cause of the sufferer's unrelenting attachment to the lost object, but also engenders an unconscious need for punishment to partially expiate the guilt, or better, to satisfy the guilt fixation.

For the critics who adapt the Freudian way of seeing to the movie, Justine improves at the movie's climactic ending because that long-deserved punishment has finally arrived in the form of the planetary collision. While the brother-in-law commits suicide and the sister cries, Justine is fully present emotionally and awaits the end with equanimity and perhaps even joy. While not all critics adopt all of the components of the Freudian theory in analyzing the film, there is a consensus that the film is "depressing," that the characters are dreadful human beings, that Justine is a deeply disturbed woman, and that it portends one eccentric but talented director's vision of the end of the world.

While the Freudian interpretation is true to the facts of the movie in the sense that the existing facts can be "seen" in a way that makes them consistent with the theory, the interpretation is, in my opinion, completely wrong. To my way of seeing, Justine's reactions to the alienation and dehumanization of her social environment are understandable and even courageous, although because she is presented to us as socially absorbed into this world—as a kind of passively willing participant in her dreadful wedding ceremony—she is far more isolated and far crazier as a result than she would have been had she instead, say, joined the women's movement or Occupy Wall Street. But considering the pathological social place in which she found herself as a thoroughly isolated woman, it was obvious to me that she was throwing all of herself into her resistance to what was being made of her from the outside. Her recovery during the course of the movie as a result of the approach of the planet, to my eyes, manifested her emergence into mental health because the arrival of the errant planet would liberate both her and also all of humanity from the social alienation, brutality, and inauthenticity into which our world had fallen. In a beautiful final scene, it is Justine who can reassure her little nephew of his security in the magic cave they construct out of sticks because this magic cave, in which Justine, her nephew, and her sister hold hands as the end approaches, is a new little world of authenticity and love and spiritual recovery of their simple common humanity. I left the theater with a full heart and a smile that I could not get off of my face, and I felt that my true self—the authentic longings of my soul—had been recognized and confirmed by Justine's final beauty and presence in the face of death and of the limits of existence itself. We really are here together if only we will embrace one another.

Now, as I say, there is nothing wrong with the Freudian theory, or the related "the movie-is-depressing" theory, on its use of the facts. Exactly the problem of all mistaken but well-articulated theories about the meaning of social events is that they express a way of seeing that *fits the facts*. What is wrong with these theories is not that that they cannot explain things, but rather that they *can* explain them and that they do so incorrectly. The error in these incorrect or faulty or too-limited ways of seeing is that rather than illuminate the meaning of social events as they actually are, they impose upon these events an order that renders this true meaning invisible.

For example, Marxism does a brilliant job of presenting historical events through a theory, a way of seeing, that fits the facts of these events. In Marx's own works and the many works that have followed in his tradition, we see the myths of various historical periods penetrated by a critical way of seeing that shows the shaping power of underlying economic factors, the hidden organization of society adapted in each epoch to the production and distribution of material goods under conditions of material scarcity. As soon as this organization produces a surplus, it is appropriated by the class of people that has gained power within a particular means of production, generating a struggle for survival between classes that is obscured by universal myths and rationalizations—ideologies—that legitimize the status quo and cover up what's really going on. In the Marxist framework, its way of seeing, everything is accounted for: economics, law, religion, culture, gender roles, racism, conquest and domination of other cultures, everything.

But Marxism is nevertheless "wrong," not because it cannot explain events, but because the superimposition of this way of seeing on historical events is not true to what we might call the social being of the events as they really are, in their being. Yes, there is a formation of classes, there is a competitive division of labor, there is appropriation of the economic surplus in unjust ways, there are masking ideologies that rationalize unjust social relations and transform might into right… but this turns out not to be taking place because of the material struggle for survival but because of a Fear of the Other that has been injected into history and reproduced across generations in ways not reducible to material factors alone, or even primarily. Yet if you come to believe in the Marxist way of seeing, if you are understandably seduced by how brilliantly it fits the facts while appealing to your instinctive sense that the world as it is is profoundly unjust, then you will be led in wrong directions by it—for example, you may think that an economic revolution that reorganizes productive relations is the key element to overcoming injustice and fulfilling human possibilities. Since coercion may be involved in such a process, that mistaken way of seeing—adopted with the best of intentions— may lead to tragic and even terrible consequences.

Nothing that I say should be understood to minimize the human suffering manifested in the history of class society—the suffering from poverty, material inequality, exploitation of economic resources and human labor, and the illegitimate hierarchies through which rulers in each historical period have dominated the ruled. Nor do I mean to minimize the human need for food, shelter, and other elements of basic material survival which continue to cause suffering for much of the world's population—for example, the 2.5 billion people who cannot obtain enough food to receive adequate nutrition each day, according to United Nations estimates. Rather what I am saying is that these forms of material suffering and injustice are manifestations of our historical legacy of our alienation from one another—that the "cause" is to be found in the social-spiritual separation expressive of an underlying failure of mutual recognition that expresses itself existentially as Fear of the Other.

Or consider Marxism's main historical competitor in the last two hundred years and its at least temporary conqueror on the historical stage, liberal individualism, and its political corollary, liberal democracy. In liberalism, we are given a way of seeing in which the social world in front of us is perceived as a vast collection of individuals, each pursuing his or her own chosen destiny, each free and equal to all the others, who combine to form collective life through private agreements and through one great public agreement, the social contract that is formed and realized through the act of voting in public elections. Within the liberal worldview, it's acknowledged that we are each born into families and must be nurtured properly through contact with others in order to achieve our individuation, our unique and sane and mature stature as individual participants in the liberal social order; but the outcome of good-enough child-rearing is self-evidently the production of the separate and free actor, who can believe whatever he or she wishes and do whatever he or she wants as long as this free action does not involve improper interference with others through improper deception or duress or other forms of coercion. Material inequalities are explained by variations in ability or the luck of the draw, but the main point here is that whatever aspects of social life might be considered unfulfilling or unjust in liberal society can eventually be solved by the system itself: Because it is the free choice of the collection of individuals themselves that will determine the existence of this lack of fulfillment or injustice, if they want to they will eventually—actually as soon as possible considering the commonsense challenges that confront human life with limited knowledge—do something about it. If we destroy the planet through nuclear war or environmental destruction, this would not invalidate the liberal worldview—it would simply reveal, with pathos, that human individuals are too burdened with inherent limitations, understood as expressions of evil or ignorance or simply biological or psychological frailties, to make a success of our own destiny as individual beings. The result of the liberal calculus would be simply that we tried and failed, but not that we had the wrong theory, that we were blinded by an incorrect way of seeing what had been going on.

Like Marxism, liberalism fits the facts perfectly; it can account for the feeling of personhood, social formations, economic life, the existence of law and government, the justifications for collective actions of all kinds, including war and environmental destruction, criminal conduct, personal unhappiness, and so on ad infinitum. The problem with liberalism is not that it doesn't fit the facts, but rather that it does fit the facts, and by doing just this obscures the true reality of the totality of phenomena that it projects itself onto. We are not actually each individuals thrown amidst a vast collection of other individuals that as a mere collection comprise the social world, the world of social existence, but are rather mutually constituting social beings perpetually knitting each other together through the inter-experience of mutual recognition into a fabric of interrelatedness that is social through and through. The reason that we feel so much like individualized entities is that we have inherited from prior generations a Fear of the Other, a fear of one another, that envelops us in the illusion of separation at a distance. While we can be grateful to liberalism and those who helped to build a world based on it for helping us to overcome the limitations of other earlier ways of seeing that caused often terrible human suffering and social injustice—ways of seeing such as the Divine Right of Kings, the natural superiority of the aristocracy, the superiority of the white race, the superiority of men over women, or of straights over gays—it is important to see that its very completeness as a social theory functions to render invisible the cause of our isolation and despair, our pathological destruction of the natural world, our infliction of starvation on the 20,000 people (many of them children) who die on the planet from lack of food every day, our imminent danger of obliterating each other with nuclear weapons that persists each day, all as if these were inevitable consequences of the way things are and have to be.

This book is one expression of a worldwide effort now taking place to bring another theory, another "way of seeing," to the forefront of human life. The central aspect of this new post-liberal, post-Marxist way of seeing is to begin from the interior of our awareness to grasp the "within" of the intersubjective life-world into which we have been thrown and into which we are, in the words of philosopher Martin Heidegger, always already in-mixed. What we find by this interior-to-interior method—from beginning inside ourselves and from that interior self-transparency going forward by intuition and understanding to the inside of the world we are trying to see—is that human beings actually exist in a psycho-spiritual world in which they seek not primarily food, shelter, or the satisfaction of material needs, but rather the love and recognition of other human beings, and the sense of elevated meaning and purpose that comes from bringing that world of intersubjective connection into being. Of course the satisfaction of material needs is indispensable to our physical survival, but please see that our survival is different from our existence—our survival is the background, the indispensable precondition of our existence, and if it is threatened we can be driven to whatever extreme is necessary to preserve this existence. But our existence itself is a manifestation of our social being that a) is fully present to itself and others, and b) exists only by virtue of our relation to the presence of others as the source of our completion. When I say that we are social beings, therefore, I mean that we do not really exist as individuals except to the extent that our individuality is one pole of our existence in relation to others, and the central longing of our life, immanent within our very existence as social beings, is to be fully recognized by the other in an embrace of love and to recognize that other with the same grace. Insofar as we must maintain the preconditions of our existence, we are motivated by the material need for survival, but our existence itself is animated by the desire to realize ourselves as social beings through connection with others, through the grace of love and mutual recognition.

Taken to the level of an overall social theory, this way of seeing—a way of seeing that bridges the interior of the social person to the interior of that person's surrounding (or historical) group—produces some core insights about social life that shape the perspective in the essays that follow on law, politics, public policy, and culture. Let me summarize the first two of these insights here, although the full development of these ideas will require another book.

First, we are all animated by the desire for mutual recognition, for a transparent connection to others in which we become fully present to each other, anchored in each other's gaze in much the way that the German theologian Martin Buber described in his book *I and Thou*. I aspire to see you and to exist in relation to you not as a mere "you over there," as a mere passing or glancing presence going by, but as a full presence both there and here, the very completion of myself insofar as we emerge into a We that is neither fleeting nor in danger of dissolving back into reciprocal solitudes corroded by mistrust and fear. The We is not a fusion or erasure of the individual person, but a realization or completion of the social person in authentic reciprocity.

Second, the world that we have been born into and have inherited is primarily characterized by the denial of this desire for mutual recognition, in the sense that we are primarily in flight from each other and experience each other as a threat. But the threat that we experience is not of "destruction" in the Darwinian or even Marxist sense of a struggle for material resources, but rather the threat of nonrecognition or ontological humiliation. When we pass each other with blank gazes on the street, punctuated by furtive steals of a passing look, our entire existential state as social beings is revealed to us—namely, that we are each, or both, encapsulated in solitude because we are pulled outward and toward each other by the desire for mutual recognition (the furtive glances *toward* each other that we each experience as compulsory), and at the same time feel compelled to deny this desire and look away—"keep our distance"—because of the immanent anxiety that the other will not reciprocate this desire for mutual recognition. This denial of our core need and desire as social beings for essential authentic reciprocity, for love in its deepest sense of essential affirmation and sight, is actually what creates the massive material injustice that Marxism and its allied ways of seeing correctly name and analyze—it is our social alienation taken as a collective totality that creates and reproduces the worldwide socioeconomic system.

Were the populations of the world not infected with this legacy of fear of nonrecognition and humiliation by the other, we would really without great difficulty solve the material problems that generate so much unnecessary suffering and pain. In other words, the world is the way it is not because people want power or wealth or control over material things, but because they cannot experience their deeper longing for love, for authentic vulnerability and recognition, and for the coming-into-presence that would be the healing of this legacy and the transcendence of it. It is our alienation that causes material injustice rather than the converse, and it is in giving birth to a new politics that overcomes our alienation that we will overcome material inequality and injustice. But such a new form of politics can emerge only from a new way of seeing that makes our social-spiritual alienation visible in perception, thought, and reflection.

Take a moment to consider the roles and masks that we feel compelled first to don and then to permanently inhabit—think of the newscaster, the weatherman, the president of the United States, this man dressed in one uniform or that woman dressed in another, the father, the therapist, the lawyer, and so forth. Although of course we can embody these roles in a way that is infused with our authentic presence, insofar as we are alienated from each other, or in a kind of flight from each other's recognition, these roles become artificial holograms of being, pseudo-manifestations of our sociality in which we seek to master and deflect the other's presence by "playing the role" from a conditioned outside that we are continually monitoring from within with an anxiety signal when we veer from it. In this mode of what the psychiatrist R.D. Laing called the "divided self," we deny our own desire for authentic intersubjective connection by throwing up the role or mask that we have been over a lifetime coerced into identifying with on pain of loss of what social connection there is, while threatening the other with a comparable erasure should he or she seek to become present as a Thou. Why do we constantly threaten each other so? Because any other course of action requires a vulnerability to the other that risks the ontological humiliation of not being recognized, of not being loved and accepted and affirmed in our existence when we are utterly laid bare as longing for that recognition and love and affirmation before the other's power to grant it or withhold it.

This leads me to five additional core insights produced by the spiritual way of seeing that I am proposing:

1. The denial of the desire for mutual recognition is not merely something that is transmitted between two persons—between you and me as we pass each other on the street—but is rather a vast, rotating social field, in which every furtive glance and blank gaze and nonpresent (elusive) role-performance is taken as what's real by each of us as we experience it. Or to put this slightly differently, every such act of flight from each other, every false way of being designed to conceal our true longing, is coupled with an implicit meta-statement that "this is who I really am" and "this is who you must recognize me as and who you really should and must be yourself." Pre-reflectively and more or less instantly, we are each perpetually internalizing the social reality and necessity of what the other is transmitting to us, and we then—in what I am calling a "rotating" fashion—re-externalize toward others as real what we have internalized from the others passing us or surrounding us emerging in and out of our social field, from infancy forward, because the social field of the whole of existence, of the life-world in which we coexist, forms a mutually influencing circle that is our conditioning. I call this aspect of our social reality the "circle of collective denial" that keeps us spiritually imprisoned in our separation, a circle that each of us co-creates because as social beings actually constituted by each other, we cannot but externalize what we have internalized even as we long to and struggle to transcend it.

2. Seen in this light, all of social life as we have inherited it thus far is a legacy of social alienation that separates us, rotating through the circle of collective denial and manifested in an infinite number of historical forms, but that we are constantly simultaneously seeking to transcend in the fullness of mutual recognition, in the simple completion of love that every newborn child anticipates at birth and manifests in the pure joyful, anticipatory presence in his or her eyes. History is, therefore, not a straight developmental process, but rather a spiral of social being, in which up to this time the desire for mutual recognition has occasionally broken through the constraints of denial of that desire that seek to contain it, erupting into social movements that ricochet across the globe often very

rapidly in a great spirit of hope and optimism. At these moments the spiral whirls upward and forward and a true revolution of our social existence becomes possible, the word "revolve" referring in reality to the turning outward of our withdrawn state toward finally grounding each other in the fullness of our reciprocal presence. And at every moment, in every interaction and social encounter, this breakthrough subtends the moment as a potentiality. But the weight of the past, and its claim on our loyalty to past patterns of safer and more impoverished forms of recognition, also at every moment work to keep us sealed in what I elsewhere have called "The Pact of the Withdrawn Selves." We have formed vast hierarchies of disciplinary control of our social presence that we call the class system, or the legal system, or family values, or an infinity of other macro and micro examples from the schools to corporations, whose limiting, unconscious spiritual aim is to contain the impulse toward the social fulfillment of mutual recognition and the vulnerability and threat of humiliation attendant to it.

3. Insofar as we each experience this internal conflict between the desire for mutual recognition and the need to deny this very desire, for fear of nonrecognition by the other and the vulnerability attendant to it, we collectively conspire to form imaginary group identities that simultaneously provide us with a sense of substitute connection or community and serve to reinforce our collective denial—or better, to seal off our longing for the authentic mutuality of I and Thou in community by an allegiance to an imaginary community that both substitutes for and encloses/represses that authentic longing. Here I am speaking of the "inflated balloon" variety of patriotism, nationalism, ethnic purity, sexual or gender identity, profession-ism—really any form of imaginary group cohesion that conceals (or more accurately, *reveals by concealing*) an inner absence of presence, a hole at the center of the imaginary group's collective being.

In my essay entitled "The Meaning of the Holocaust: Social Alienation and the Infliction of Human Suffering" (*The Bank Teller*, Chapter 2), I show the way this type of imaginary identity emerged within Nazi Germany as an inflation of an illusory imago of community concealing an inner terror of humiliation, the goal of which was precisely to conceal the vulnerability to that anticipated threat that existed *inside* the puffed-up, grandiose Nazi imago of unity and connection. And I show in historical context how each person given over to the illusory bond of the imago makes allegiance to this false unity compulsory on all others, in the service of sealing off the deeper longing for and fear of true recognition—in such a manner that no one is allowed to see the bond's illusory nature because it is manifested as "real." Even more, when the collective imago is inflated to this extent, it is also manifested as "perfect" to prevent any challenge to it—not to maintain the validity of the imago as such, but to seal off the vulnerability to the longing that underlies it. While the Nazi situation was the extreme and perhaps limiting example of what I am describing, this impoverishment of social being is manifested also in the way, say, boys in my childhood behaved in the locker room in aspiring to their male identities, or the way the corporate lawyer carries his briefcase and speaks too loudly at the meeting ("We lawyers" speak as if we're in charge)—in other words, in all forms of false social unity in which we as social persons co-construct a carapace or shell of ungrounded or artificial social connection that both covers over and seals off the true being that underlies and also unconsciously observes and monitors it.

4. The giving over of our social being, in alienation, to the false group is always accompanied by what is commonly called the demonization of the other, in which the always-experienced threat of dissolution of the false group, which is at every moment unstable because it is in fact illusory and sustained by the requirement of compulsory allegiance only, is channeled into a projection out on to some Other that supposedly is the true source of the threat to the group's artificial unity. Whether it is the Jews, the gays, the blacks, the women, the students, the unions, or, to use the Dr. Seuss example that I use in one of the essays in this book, the people who butter their toast on the bottom instead of the top, these others are sacrificed not because they are actual human beings who are rejected and expelled for their true nature, but because they are turned into carriers of the threat that inhabits and corrodes the false group itself, the threat of its own unmasking. The false group, an illusory unity of communion, always defends itself against exposure by pretending that some projected other is a threat to its solidity and infinite continuation, when the true threat is exposure of the underlying vulnerability to a longing too painful to acknowledge. The choice of the particular carrier of this threat is always shaped by historical conditions—like the legacy of anti-Semitism in Germany in the case of the Nazis—but the underlying dynamic is a characteristic of social alienation itself: an imaginary group cannot sustain itself without a demonized other because it must by its very nature as

imaginary, as illusory, as false, have a projected outlet to enable it to continually master and conceal its own artificiality.

5. Finally, and this is of central importance to the optimism and moral direction—let me call it the moral optimism—that I hope comes through in what I write here, this entire description of the process of social alienation that accounts for so much human suffering is at every moment countered by the desire to transcend it, by the inherent goodness of every human being that codetermines and transcends the way each of us manifests our presence in every moment of our existence. Here again please recall the presence of every newborn child during the first years of life, the full presence of the child's radiance and life-force as it is manifested in the child's whole way of being, in the full eyes, in the spontaneity of its gestures and reaching out, in the search for the other's loving gaze and embrace and its willingness to make whatever meaningful sounds we make ("language") to be *with* us. This new-born being we always remain, underneath the legacy of our alienated conditioning. What my friend Michael Lerner and I (and now many others) call "spiritual activism" is collective activism for social change that seeks through practical, present-day actions to make manifest our deep longing for spiritual connection and to partially realize that connection through a new form of spiritual politics. For example, the Network of Spiritual Progressives that I am a part of aspires to and presses for universal health care not simply because we need doctors to care for our bodies, but because universal health care is a necessary manifestation of our universal longing to recognize and care for each other's well-being and that of each other's families and loved ones, as well as to be similarly cared for ourselves: health care means *caring about each other's health*. Social Security is important not simply because older people need financial help as they age, but as a manifestation of intergenerational love and solidarity that elevates the communal self-presence of the entire society. In these senses, as I say in the early essays on law in this book, I embrace Martin Luther King's definition of justice as "love correcting that which revolts against love."

As I hope the last two brief examples demonstrate, the theory of social being and social existence that I am summarizing here is therefore not a theory that is "merely psychological" and divorced from the real world's problems and struggles. It is as fully engaged with the socio-economic and political struggles of the world as, say, Marxism itself. What is different about it is that it is based on a way of seeing human reality—in every social interaction between two people and in the unfolding and development of human groups as a whole—that places the spiritual dimension of social existence at the center of our understanding of social phenomena and at the center of our effort to transcend the problems that continue to limit and constrain us. While these problems certainly also have a material and economic dimension to them—the reality of children dying of starvation around the world, the lack of adequate food and housing for so many in the United States and around the world, and the vulnerability of the large majority of the world's population to having to face such material and economic difficulties mean that it is obvious that the material dimension of existence and the risk of scarcity impinges immensely on human life—this material, economic dimension is a context of the body rather than an essence of the consciousness-in-action that is social-being-in-the-world. Social existence is constituted out of the spirituality of social consciousness-in-the world, within the intersubjective flow of recognition, of love and the denial of love; and as much as the survival and well-being of the physical body is central to the context of the unfolding of this social inter-experience, across history and in the present moment, any theory or way of seeing that focuses primarily on this material element as the central descriptive or explanatory factor is missing the essence of social being itself as a manifestation of the human spirit and its struggle to fully realize itself, always in social form.

The above is a summary of the theory, or "way of seeing," that informs the essays in this book, but the theory is only rarely emphasized explicitly in the essays. As was the case in my earlier book *The Bank Teller*, the theory is rather taken for granted in the descriptions that constitute the essays: law and justice; politics as the human co-creation of the world through elections and other forms of group formation; public policy in the context of how to think about war and peace, gay rights and sexual identity, and the spiritual foundations of science; and finally the meaning of cultural phenomena, from the work of one great philosopher influential to me (Jean-Paul Sartre), to baseball, to photography, to living with illness as a cultural reality. The essays, in other words, are applications of the theory to a wide variety of real-life examples rather than explications of the theory itself. It is in the nature of the intersubjective, spiritual-political theory that I am proposing that its truth-value to you depends upon whether you can recognize it as true rather than any analytical proof or capacity to explain diverse facts that is the measure of the truth of more scientific ways of seeing and thinking.

All phenomenological or descriptive theory depends not upon a theory's ability to explain facts from premises or theoretical postulates, but rather upon its self-evidence, upon its capacity to produce an experience of recognition in the reader. Since the theory itself begins with a social-spiritual understanding of the very thing that the theory is addressing and talking about, the only claim to validity that it can make upon the reader is the extent to which the reader can recognize it as adequate to fully *reveal* what is being described. While a descriptive theory can be true even if nobody understands it or recognizes it as true, it can become a valid form of social knowledge only through its capacity to generate an experience of recognition in a reader who him- or herself shares the very being of the "object of the investigation," of the thing being talked about.

That is why, in both *The Bank Teller* and in this book, I have written essays about very practical matters like (in the former) a bank teller caught in a corporate hierarchy, the relationship between imaginary forms of community and the holocaust, the limitations of Darwin's theory of evolution, the relationship of the sixties to the rise of Ronald Reagan, the meaning of a Maalox commercial—and in this book, the constitution and the legal system, John Kerry's and Barack Obama's "presence" (or the lack of it), the war in Iraq, sexual fear and gay marriage, opening day at a Giants-Dodgers game. Each essay is meant to illuminate a world that I "see" through the lens of the theory—the way of perceiving and then thinking and describing—that I have presented in summary form above.

The organization of the essays in this book, as was also largely true in the last, presents the essays both according to theme (Law, Politics, Public Policy, and Culture) and in chronological order within each theme or part. I have presented the essays for the most part chronologically, because I am trying to apply my spiritual-political way of seeing not only to diverse subject areas—to show how it is helpful for understanding the world as a whole in its diverse manifestations—but also to show through the chronology of the essays the historical development of the phenomena I describe, especially in the area of politics and public policy to the extent that the policy issues themselves occur in an historical frame. If the two books are read together, I hope readers can see the historical development of the vicissitudes of mutual recognition … its social flow and blockage in the context of a quite volatile, ongoing, historically specific struggle of hope against fear … as this struggle has unfolded from the 1950s through the present moment in 2013, from JFK through Barack Obama as embodied expressions of precisely these spiritual-political flows-in-tension as they have been manifested through political leaders, and in the area of public policy from, for example, the rise of creationism as part of the New Right to the emergence of other more emancipatory spiritual approaches to science some twenty years later and the relationship of both (as reaction-formation in the case of creationism, as continuation of the liberatory impulse in the case of the sacred biologists) to the breakthrough of recognition that actually was the 1960s.

In my lifetime, it has been primarily the movements of the 1960s that have generated the upward spiral of hope and authentic mutual recognition in the historical process, just as the 1930s did so for the generation that preceded mine. During the period from roughly 1965-1974, a parallel awareness emerged in the United States and ricocheted across the world very rapidly, a propulsion of spiritual presence that provided people like me with a new ground to stand our lives on. For precisely this reason, because of the threat posed to traditional and more alienated forms of connection that nevertheless were also conditions of social membership and spiritual safety, the 1960s and the parallel ontological universe it gave birth to also have generated a powerful defensive social reaction— in Freudian terms, the reaction that the superego, in defense of the ego, always has to the transcendent longings of the id. Within the social-spiritual way of seeing the world, the upward movement of history is carried forward by such breakthroughs, or to recall the Doors, by breaking on through to the other side of the system of blocked connection. And these breakthroughs are never fully forgotten in historical consciousness, even as they are resisted through coerced deference to artificial conditioning, disciplinary observation, cooptation, flight into irony, and direct violence, among other expressions of the legacy of our alienation from our true loving selves.

The essays in this book are meant as an effort to help preserve the spiritual insight afforded to my generation by an upsurge of the human spirit more powerful than the force, existing not in Them but within each of us, that is trying to contain it. One expression of that spiritual upsurge, that outbreak of social connection, is the way of seeing social being and historical social life that I try to give voice to here. Like Marxism and liberalism, I believe that the descriptions in these essays fit the facts of the realities they describe, but in a way that I hope is truer to the social reality that they describe because of the inclusion of the spiritual-political dimension that the 1960s made visible in my lifetime and that may prefigure the kind of seeing and thinking that will provide a basis for the next movement upward to change the world.

—PETER GABEL

San Francisco, California
July, 2013

PART ONE

LAW AND JUSTICE

THE IDEAS IN THE INTRODUCTION have a personal quality: the desire for mutual recognition, the denial of that desire in alienated interactions; the invention of and attachment to imaginary communities as substitute forms of human connection; the demonization of others as a protection of the false self against humiliation—all of these concepts tend to refer us to our own subjective experience. But inherent in the notion that activism has an essential spiritual dimension is the idea that the desire for authentic connection and the blockage or deflection or evasion of that desire are social truths pervading the whole of our social world, the public "outer" sphere as well the private sphere of personal relations. Spiritual activism describes the effort to affect the world in a way that opens up and elevates our collective consciousness, that seeks to heal and overcome not merely the alienation that separates I and Thou and even a third and a fourth, but rather the alienation affecting the social world as a whole insofar as that world is colored by or really imprisoned in social separation. This means that the splits that we normally employ in describing the inner and the outer, the private and the public, must be overcome if we are to see the spiritual reality of our social existence as it really is, as a rotating flow of *inter*-subjectivity of which our personal interactions and experience form only a part—or better still, of which our personal interactions and experience are merely one expression.

The essays on law that open this book ask the reader to see law through a new lens that reveals this link between the personal world and the socio-political world. As the opening essay "Imagine Law" indicates, law is not correctly pictured as a "body of rules" distributing thing-like rights and duties to abstract citizens, but is rather a culture of justice in which the moral and spiritual dimension of human relations is given expression through ideas, images, and public rituals like courtroom hearings and trials, including the uniforms worn, the roles enacted, and the signifying of the world itself as it is pictured through legal discourse. To the degree that we accept, through the medium of law and legal culture, an authoritative world-picture that represents us as socially separated citizens with boundaries marked by bundles of "rights," we participate in a way of seeing our common existence that may minimize or even entirely erase *a priori* the spiritual and moral bonds that unite us. And to the extent that we are conditioned from birth to "believe in" this authoritative picture, we prevent ourselves from becoming aware of what we are excluding—we become unconscious actors trapped in the wrong play.

The essays on law in Part One try to make the unconscious conscious by channeling the spiritual awareness we normally associate with personal life into the public legal realm, by revealing the limitations of the legal world as we currently conceive it, and by intimating a new and possible legal world—a world connecting love and justice—that we can begin to create once we become conscious of the inherited concept of law that envelops us. Two of the essays—"Law and Hierarchy" and "Critical Legal Studies as a Spiritual Practice"—were written as part of my work within the Critical Legal Studies (CLS) movement in legal scholarship, which itself emerged from the social movements of the 1960s as some of us shaped by the sixties became law professors in the seventies. Critical Legal Studies ultimately became primarily an expression of the prevailing interest in deconstruction and postmodernism, which in CLS was manifested as an effort to show the indeterminate and therefore inherently political nature of legal reasoning, obscuring the work of those of us who were developing a spiritual critique of existing legal culture as an expression of social alienation which pointed toward the creation of a new legal culture that would link true justice with social healing and authentic mutual recognition. The two essays about CLS included here represent the road not taken and try to reopen it as a path for a new generation of legal scholars and activists.

ESSAY ONE

IMAGINE LAW

THE MOST PROFOUND DEFINITION OF JUSTICE is Martin Luther King Jr.'s: "Love correcting that which revolts against Love." Its power comes from its affirmation that we are first of all connected, that as individuals we are but unique incarnations of a spiritual force that unites us, and that justice is the making manifest of that love by correcting, through the inherent ethical call that this love makes upon every one of us and all of us, the spiritual distortions that revolt against love and seek to deny it. It was to this inherent ethical understanding emanating from the very essence of our social existence, pulling upon the conscience of the oppressor as much as giving courage to the oppressed, that King always addressed himself. Injustice is as self-evident to us as the presence of justice—even the Nazi cannot stop killing for fear of becoming aware of what he knows—and it is the necessity of love that both enables us to tell justice from injustice and calls upon us to move from the one to the other.

Law ought to be the particular temporal embodiment of our effort as a real historical community to move from the one to the other. Law is not a body of rules or any other such thing-like entity, but rather a culture of justice whose ethical legitimacy depends upon how deeply and sincerely it enables us to carry out the work of justice, of love correcting that which revolts against love. Thus conceived, legal culture ought to be a spiritual practice through which the community calls upon love's evolving wisdom to heal the spiritual distortions that continue to alienate us from love itself as the realization of our social being. Like the mountain climber who first throws his pick up to the top of the mountain, making sure that the pick is anchored so as to maximize the tension in his rope, and who then seeks to pull himself upward by intuitively gauging the rightness of every step in relation to his ultimate and transcendent end, law must maintain its connection to justice by following an ethical intuition anchoring the present to the future, an intuition of what we are in our being but are not yet in reality.

America's legal culture at the turn of the millennium has temporarily lost this connection to justice because its great historical accomplishment—the affirmation of the freedom of the individual and the protection of the individual from officially sanctioned group coercion—has been misunderstood to require the denial of the spiritual bond that unites the individual to the other and, through love, fulfills the individual in his or her social existence. As a result, alongside the accomplishments of constitutional democracy and the Bill of Rights, which liberated the individual from the officially sanctioned religious and political oppression of previous historical periods, we have created a society of disconnected monads, spiritually isolated and starved for love and recognition. Not only has this collective spiritual starvation now progressed to the point of posing a threat to the very existence of the planet (because the denial of the universal need for loving connection has spawned a pathological, paranoiac scramble to exploit everything outside oneself—other people and the natural world—in order to "save" oneself), it has also failed to secure the liberty of the individual in whose name the denial of our spiritual bond was legislated. Today as "free individuals," we live most of our lives in a completely unnecessary spiritual prison, each of us longing for the same liberation that only we can provide each other, each of us denying that this longing exists within ourselves because we doubt that our longing would or could be reciprocated by the other.

Let us begin by acknowledging that it is we, and not merely Eleanor Rigby, who are all the lonely people, withdrawn into our heads and peering out at a social world whose collective gaze we have come to fear and whose love, whose reciprocating acceptance and affirming recognition, is at the same time our only spiritual salvation.

Of course the law is not exclusively to blame for this, but it does have a special responsibility because it legitimizes our predicament in the name of justice. Law cannot exist without claiming to be just: it would be superfluous to elevate what are merely orders backed by the threat of violence to some higher cultural status. But when law loses its true spiritual connection to justice, it becomes "legitimation"—a justification of the status quo that lacks the ethical legitimacy that only moral anchorage in true justice, Martin Luther King's justice, can provide. Law as legitimation exploits the longing for justice by using the claim of justice to legitimate an alienated society that the community, deep in its core, experiences as spiritually and ethically illegitimate.

Thus however much we are tempted to blame the present ecological and spiritual crisis on the global capitalist marketplace, for example, we must realize that this marketplace is held in place, so to speak, by a legal culture that through a vast network of "rights" allows the community of souls that form that marketplace to believe that what it is doing is right and even required by justice itself. If the prevailing culture of justice declares that individual liberty means there exists no spiritual force, no essential love, that unites us to each other and to the sacredness of the natural world and the wider universe, then the universal longings of the soul are in contradiction with the community's public declaration—through the official political and legal institutions that define the community's very public existence—of the ethical basis of community membership. To put it simply, absent the support of a spiritual/cultural/political movement, the isolated soul cannot but believe that its longing for a loving and spiritually connected society is "wrong" and that the ethics of the marketplace is both "right" and a condition of social membership. Thus the prevailing legal culture, which we begin to internalize even before the explicit conditioning of seventh and eighth-grade civics class, plays a unique and powerful role not only in sustaining what is, but in keeping our spiritual longings and our spiritual knowledge a collective and even unconscious secret.

Since what we are to imagine, in a moment, is precisely the legal/spiritual revolution that will dissolve these invisible walls that separate us, we must first enumerate the elements of our existing legal culture that contribute to this state of affairs and that must be revolutionized. All of these elements reflect the central mistaken conviction that the protection of individual liberty requires the denial of, rather than the affirmation of, the spiritual bond that unites us. Here are the most important ones:

1. Our legal culture declares that disputes are to be resolved through an adversary system that defines differences as antagonistic clashes of conflicting interests, fosters hostility, mutual deprecation, and lying, and rejects any moral objective that might inform the process beyond the parties' own objectives, beyond their self-interested goals. Protection of the "rights of the individual" is thought to require that each side treat the other with skepticism and mistrust, to demean the other's position while exaggerating the virtue of your own, to use cross-examination to undermine the testimony of even those you believe to be truthful, and to conceal any information that might be harmful to your side unless your opponent extracts it from you under penalty of perjury (only in rare circumstances is voluntary disclosure legally required). The adversary process assumes that justice is best served by the use of evidentiary rules that limit what the judge and jury may hear to the proof of empirically verifiable facts. Any evidence regarding the spiritual and social meaning of the dispute or of the social and ethical context that might bring out this meaning is inadmissible because it is regarded

as "merely subjective," merely matters of opinion that cannot be determined to be true or untrue and therefore can only unfairly prejudice the objectivity of the proceeding. The assumption is that the vindication of "individual rights" is the basis of law's claim to justice, and that objectivity in pursuit of that end is best assured by having an impartial third-party (sometimes the judge, sometimes a jury) evaluate each side's case after the other has had a full opportunity to destroy it.

2. Once the "facts" are thus determined, the basic rules of substantive law that are used to resolve disputes—embodied in, for example, the law of contracts, torts, corporations, and property— assume that people are essentially unconnected monads whose principal desire is to pursue their own material self-interest in the competitive marketplace, and whose principal social concern is limited to protecting their persons and property against unwanted interference by others. Even the Constitution, often thought to be among the world's great documents in securing social justice, provides no recognition of the human longing for community, for social connection, for the authenticity of mutual recognition, for the creation of a society that fosters our awareness of the sacredness of life itself and of the natural world. Instead, the main text of the Constitution provides only the formal structure to secure a democracy of strangers, an unconnected collection of individuals protected against their neighbors by the secret ballot and against abuses by the government itself through the "checks and balances" secured by the separation of powers. Similarly, the Bill of Rights does not aspire to connect us to one another but to protect us against each other, against the community's interfering with our right as isolated individuals to speak, to assemble (if as disconnected monads we can find anyone to assemble with), to be secure in our homes (those supposed havens in a heartless world), and even to keep others from taking away our guns. Indeed, the current preoccupation with "the right to bear arms" is an example of a highly visible appeal to the Bill of Rights (in this case the Second Amendment) that reveals how clearly its protections equate individual freedom with fear of the other rather than connection with and love for the other.

3. In their training and in the disciplinary and ethical rules that govern the legal profession, lawyers are encouraged and even to some extent required to ignore ethical considerations beyond the narrow self-

interest of the client. Because our legal culture lacks a spiritual and moral direction, or more precisely because it denies the legitimacy of embracing such a direction in order to defend an isolated conception of individual liberty, the role of the lawyer is simply to advocate for the legitimacy of whatever the client wants or does (so long as it is not a crime). Legal education is almost exclusively directed toward teaching students the analytical techniques of rule-manipulation; the best students are those who can demonstrate their capacity to argue for any side irrespective of moral consequences. No part of a law student's education is directed toward instilling in the student the obligation or the capability to promote the creation of a more loving, more spiritually whole society. And once in practice, the lawyer's professional "duty of zealous representation" virtually requires the lawyer not to allow his or her own "private" ethical concerns to interfere with the zealous pursuit of the client's ends, irrespective of the impact of these ends on others, on the society as a whole, or on the environment.

Because the individualistic, materialist, and adversarial character of this legal culture is "binding" on the consciousness of society—because its assumptions about who human beings are and how we ought to relate to one another are also The Law—we cannot overcome the spiritual alienation that is at the heart of our own and the world's suffering without a fundamental transformation of this culture. And because the great social movements of the twentieth century did not grasp this, they foundered when they entered the legal arena. The labor movement, the civil rights movement, and the women's movement, for example, were fundamentally spiritual movements aspiring to a new kind of connection that would realize our common humanity—even the word "movement" denotes the spiritual emergence of just such a vitalizing connection. But once these movements began to translate their spiritual aspirations into a demand for legal rights, their very victories became a cause of the defeat of these aspirations. Absorbed into the law's individualistic and materialist framework, the labor movement's aspiration to a classless society based on solidarity and universal brotherhood became the right to bargain for higher wages and safer working conditions; the civil rights movement's aspiration to love across our racial differences became the right of "the individual" not to be discriminated against on the basis of race in order to protect his or her liberty to pursue "equality of opportunity" in the marketplace; the aspiration of the women's movement to replace a world of power, hierarchy, and heartless rationality with a communal, intuitively grounded fabric of care became the right not to have one's liberty to pursue material success in the marketplace impeded by gender. No matter how important these liberal victories were, they required looking in a mirror that made the spiritual aspiration for a fundamental social transformation invisible.

Yet for a complex of reasons—the most important of which are probably the failure of the liberal global marketplace to create a meaningful social existence, and the failure of the movements for social transformation to be able to sustain themselves through either the liberal or the materialist-socialist framework—a new flower has begun to sprout across the face of the world. This flower is the worldwide spiritual/ecological movement that is finally helping the necessity of love to recognize itself as the spiritual force that unites us. To bring this recognition to fruition, to enable this flower to grow in spite of the centuries of alienation and mistrust and "misrecognition" that have preceded its birth into awareness, we must create a new legal culture. And we are already beginning to do so.

A legal culture that can begin to realize Dr. King's great description of justice is one in which the community's response to conflict of every kind—civil and criminal to use the current categories—begins with a moral awareness of the love, the sense of compassionate and caring social connection, that is to be restored through the legal process. This requires that law's primary focus no longer be judgment directed toward divided individuals, but the healing of wounds to the connection that is to be restored.

This in turn requires that the three principal elements of the individualistic and materialist legal culture undergo the following transformation:

1. The adversary system should be abolished and replaced by processes that encourage empathy, compassion, and mutual understanding. Each human and ecological problem that requires community resolution should proceed by locating the presentation of all "facts" within a context of social meaning that reveals their ethical significance. Within this transformed framework, the courtroom would be the public space devoted to healing the spiritual wounds of alienation by allowing the community to hear these wounds in their full human dimension, instead of restricting what constitutes "evidence" to intentionally de-spiritualized "facts." For example, imagine the effect of a single public hearing of a case of racial oppression in such a setting. Imagine if the community and the perpetrator listened with a legally validated compassion to the suffering of the victim, and then with equal compassion to the desperate allegiance of the perpetrator to whatever distorted vision of racial superiority and false communal identity led him or her to

inflict humiliation and pain on another (for listening with compassion does not mean sparing the offender of moral responsibility). And imagine the healing effect on the wider culture of watching such spiritual truths revealed on television—in contrast, say, to the alienating effect of watching the manipulations of the O.J. Simpson trial. The effect of a single such act of collective witnessing would have an immense impact by giving communal recognition, through a public legal process, to the pain of separation that pervades all of our lives and produces our worst distortions.

If you find it difficult to imagine how we could arrive at such a transformed vision of law's purpose and process, consider the rapid spread of the Restorative Justice movement in criminal law in America today. All across the country concerned lawyers, religious leaders, and community members are seeking to heal the community wounds caused by crime by creating safe contexts for victims to confront those who have hurt them with the full expression of the pain they have suffered, by allowing the perpetrators to come face to face with the reality of the other that such a confrontation permits, and by sometimes eliciting sincere apologies and the sincere forgiveness that is the only true way to repair the spiritual harm of violence. Of course these restorative justice processes also require the offender to provide appropriate and meaningful restitution to the victim where possible—such as requiring, in one case, two teenagers who had defiled a Des Moines synagogue with swastikas to remove the offending symbols, perform other community service, and study Jewish history in addition to coming to understand, through face-to-face encounters with Holocaust survivors who were members of the synagogue, the enormity of the suffering associated with the swastika. But the essential point of restorative justice is responding to crime in a manner consonant with love correcting that which revolts against love, with understanding crime as a wound to love that is itself almost always caused by such a wound that preceded the criminal act.

The power of this re-imagining of the healing power of law has been nowhere better revealed than in the work of South Africa's Truth and Reconciliation Commission (TRC) under the leadership of Bishop Desmond Tutu. That commission sought to avoid the vengeance that almost inevitably accompanies revolutions against a legacy of oppression by seeking, on behalf of the black majority, to forgive the white minority for the crimes of apartheid so long as the offenders acknowledged the truth of what they had done. With all its limitations, including the immense political complications accompanying the TRC's work (hearing and televising a review of some 22,000 cases often involving extreme violence), the TRC is one of the greatest experiments in human history in a spiritual approach to healing social conflict. Imagine if we began now to take the next millennium to build our entire legal culture on the TRC's premise announced in the title of Bishop Tutu's recent book: *No Future Without Forgiveness*.

> 2. The role of "rules" in resolving disputes in civil cases should be greatly diminished, in favor of wisdom guided by ethical and spiritual ideals. Just as the Restorative Justice movement has sought to foster the healing of the effects of violence on individuals and communities in criminal cases, the process of resolving civil disputes should draw upon the healing-centered focus of today's transformative mediation movement to assist in the realization of these spiritual and ethical ideals.

The importance of this shift can best be understood by grasping the changes in legal culture that will have to occur for David Korten's visionary conception of a post-corporate, sustainable economy to actually come into being (*The Post-Corporate World* (1999)). Korten's alternative to globalization calls for the creation of "mindful markets" that will be based on such ethical values as true mutuality and cooperation, respect for the meaningfulness of one another's labor, the production of material goods that satisfy real human needs in a manner that respects the sacredness of the earth, and respect by economic actors for the integrity of each other's local cultures. But the only way to bring about such an economic transformation is to build a parallel legal culture that gradually helps to develop acceptance of these values as expressive of a just economy, and to fill out the practical meaning of these ideal values through the resolution of individual cases over time—through a spiritual/ethical equivalent of our present individualist/materialist common law.

What this new legal culture requires is not a new set of abstract rules to be applied neutrally and logically to strangers who want to remain strangers, but a legal process that emphasizes empathic listening and the elicitation of the social meaning of an economic exchange in order to gradually overcome the legacy of capitalist self-interest that presupposes disconnection between the parties. The purpose of the legal proceeding must be to bring into being a connection expressive of Korten's vision of an ethical and sustainable economic culture. If a dispute develops between a buyer of coffee in the United States and a supplier from Central America, the legal resolution of the dispute should perhaps begin with a period of meditation and a sharing of food and music, followed by a telling of respective stories and a period of questioning (not "cross-examination") aimed at resolving the dispute in accordance with the aspiration to a spiritual and ethical ideal. The aspiration to respect the inherent worth and meaningfulness of each other's labor cannot be realized by a verbal statement of this ideal in the form of a "rule" to which alienated actors must conform their conduct, but by a process that realizes this aspiration is an ideal "in front of us" that must be nurtured into existence through empathy, education, and reciprocal sensitivity.

Accompanying the subordination of rules to ideals in substantive law must be the development of spiritual remedies for the resolution of differences. In today's legal culture, the measure of all things is money. Consistent with the law's emphasis on material self-interest and the profit motive as the driving force of humankind, the legal remedy prescribed for almost every injury, whether economic (such as breach of contract) or non-economic (such as sexual harassment) is monetary damages to be transferred from one disconnected stranger to another. In the civil area as in the criminal area, remedies aimed at creating social connection must emphasize acknowledgment of wrong-doing and the elicitation of genuinely voluntary apology and forgiveness. Of course some and perhaps many cases will require some material restitution for material loss unjustly suffered by one party, but even here the aim wherever possible should be the promotion of future material assistance freely given, rather than just the payment of money.

Finally, while I have here emphasized re-imagining the relationship between a new legal culture and a new economic culture, the same re-imagining should occur in the non-economic sphere of a reconceived civil society that aspires to connect us rather than separate us. To take but the most obvious example, the present rule of American tort law that there is no duty to attempt to rescue someone in distress—for example, someone drowning in front of you in a swimming pool—should be replaced by the ideal expectation that we will do all we can to rescue each other from isolation, fear, and danger, whether someone is drowning or someone is homeless. That we today associate this expectation as "making sense" only in relation to intimate family members is but a result of our conditioning that transforms those outside the tiny circle of blood relations into mere strangers, mere vessels of anonymity to whom we are not essentially related.

3. The role of lawyers must be equally reconceived as a "calling" rather than a trade. Instead of lawyers understanding themselves as neutral legitimators of their clients' individual self-interest, lawyers must reconceive of themselves as healers—that is, as spiritual actors whose aim is to reconcile the goals of their clients with the creation of a loving world. No longer should the ethics of the profession encourage the criminal defense lawyer to seek the acquittal of those whom the lawyer knows has committed violent acts, or encourage the lawyer for a lumber company to help his or her client destroy

old-growth Redwoods with impunity. Instead, the lawyer should be trained from the first day in law school to engage every human situation with which he or she is confronted so as to create a better, more spiritually connected world. Rule-manipulation and the cultivation of cleverness should give way, through the study not of "cases" but of ethically compelling and challenging situations, to empathic engagement with both one's client's deepest hopes and the reconciliation of those hopes with the law's substantive ethical ideals. The purpose of the profession as a whole, therefore, should be the deepening of the collective moral consciousness of the community as a whole, as the community—finally facing the inevitability of the destruction of its own species if it cannot overcome the fear of the other that has come to dominate its existence—approaches Martin Luther King Jr.'s simple and universally desired moral truth.

Whether this vision sounds hopelessly utopian to you or fully realizable and even necessary—whether you believe such a profoundly connected vision of law and legal culture cannot be accomplished without unacceptable threats to individual freedom, or, on the other hand, whether you believe such a vision of legally recognized spiritual connection is essential to the fulfillment of individual liberation—depends upon whether you really can embrace Martin Luther King Jr.'s affirmation that loving connection made manifest in the world will be but the realization of who we already are. I can embrace this. And with Dr. King and John Lennon in my mind's eye, I know I'm not the only one.

ESSAY TWO

LAW AND HIERARCHY

WHEN DUNCAN KENNEDY PUBLISHED *Legal Education and the Reproduction of Hierarchy* in 1983, Ronald Reagan had been in office for three years, and the dominant culture's ultimately (largely) successful war against the 1960s was in full swing. But at that time our fate was not sealed, and in the world of legal education, the Critical Legal Studies movement was "hot"—the subject of serious legal symposia in the Stanford and Texas Law Reviews, a cause for extensive hand-wringing and outrage by icons of the legal establishment, the subject of major (largely denunciatory) articles in *The New Yorker*, *The New Republic*, and national newspapers concerned that the Harvard and Stanford Law Schools in particular were being taken over by radicals. We were also a source of real energy and hope for ourselves—young law professors who had been shaped by the utopian aspirations of the 1960s for a democratic and egalitarian society and who wanted to carry our insights forward toward the transformation of legal education and the whole world—as well as for the generation of law students following us who could still feel in the air the idealism, and basic rightness of that idealism, that was pulsing through us and pushing us all forward. Hundreds of people attended our annual conferences that took place at a different leading law school each year; men, women, and increasingly men and women of color engaged in intense intellectual debate during the day and danced late into the night to the Rolling Stones and Aretha Franklin; and week-long summer camps became exhilarating annual gatherings full of serious study and fun. Although the planning for them may have been in the works in some Washington think-tanks, the Federalist Societies had not yet taken their place as campus institutions, societies which were eventually publicly blessed and thanked by Mr. Reagan himself toward the end of his second term for having decisively defeated the plague to our national well-being known as Critical Legal Studies.

Duncan's "little red book" was thus flung into an historical moment ripe with

This essay was originally written for the 2004 republication of *Legal Education and the Reproduction of Hierarchy: A Polemic Against the System* by Duncan Kennedy, published by NYU Press, and is reproduced here by permission of NYU Press.

hope, and yet with storm clouds on the horizon that would eventually overwhelm us. Those storm clouds were not by any means exclusively the creation of our opponents—they were in significant part the result of the limitations of our own vision and of the movements of the sixties themselves, including our own. In my opinion, some of those limitations are reflected in Duncan's book, and I will address them momentarily. But first I want to state what is brilliant and important about the book, and how the ideas in it accurately express the relationship between the revelations unveiled by the movements of the sixties and the critique of legal education as one embodiment of the reproduction of hierarchy that, to use Duncan's word, "maims" all of us by depriving us of our capacity for freedom and collective self-determination ... as well as (and this prefigures my critique of the book) our spiritual capacity to become fully present to ourselves and to each other in relations of loving human connection and mutual recognition.

* * *

When I say that Duncan published his book in the midst of a war waged by the dominant culture against the movements of the sixties, what I mean by "war" is not primarily a struggle to control who will run the economic system or the institutions of American society, but a war over the nature of consciousness, and the nature of reality itself. The sixties was fundamentally not a movement for reform or revolution according to the inherited meaning of those words, as if what the world needed was a reordering of the external relationships of reality to make economic and political "systems" more equal, or to overthrow the power of the ruling class and replace it with some kind of externally pictured mass democracy, or anything of that kind. The movement was rather a movement of desire, of aspiration, an opening up of closed space that allowed millions of people to come to see and feel something invisible—namely, the artificiality and even unreality of the inherited world and the possibility of a better, more humane, and more real one.

Many, many forces contributed to this opening up of desire, among them the civil rights movement of the 50s, Elvis, the Beat Poets, the evocative lyricism of JFK, the insufferable lack of oxygen in the atmosphere of the post World War II kitchen culture of the 1950s. But the main factor was the Vietnam War and the growing awareness among millions of young people in particular that something insane was taking place, and it was taking place not because the war was in the economic interests of General Motors but because in some sense the whole world was out of its mind, out of touch with Being itself, living out scripts that rationalized the mass murder of millions of human beings.

There is an album from that period by a rock group called the Electric Flag that illustrates what I mean by this. The opening song begins with then-president Lyndon Johnson saying in the southern drawl that we heard every night on the news "My Fellow Americans..." followed by a few words, and then a mass of people bursting into laughter. The point was that out of the passive confusion that characterized the initial years of ambivalence toward the war, and out of the contradiction that the draft was posing for all of us of whether we were going to ... die ... because it was our "role" to do so, and out of countless televised images of human suffering and death that acquired a surreal character as all of us faced with this contradiction gradually grasped that real people and not televised images were dying without any plausible narrative intelligibility (without any story we could tell ourselves of why this made sense)—out of all this came the genuine insight that Lyndon Johnson was in some way merely playing the role of "president" and that things were happening, real events were occurring, that were the outcome of large masses of people all playing one role or another in the reproduction of a society that was unable to stop this war precisely because they were entrapped in these roles.

I say that this insight was an expression of the opening up of desire because it emerged through a liberating process of mutual discovery, in which each of us was suddenly brought into a palpably more authentic contact with others through a dawning "shock of recognition." Out of the drifty isolation of our passive conditioning, in which we were to simply play out the passive roles assigned to us by accident of birth and the cultural predestinations that followed from our class, race, gender, and a multitude of other social attributes, we suddenly felt galvanized into a movement of more connected and more real human beings who could, must, actively shape a more authentic destiny for ourselves and a more just and loving world. Through this phenomenal ricochet of mutual recognition that spread rapidly across the entire face of the earth, what had been invisible became visible and a kind of authentic, elevating love and joy spread across the psycho-spiritual energy field that was social existence itself. That turning of the spirit outward toward the other is the true meaning of the word "movement," since of course nobody physically moves anywhere except during demonstrations or when dancing to music.

But this process of revelation did not instantly change the inherited world and its institutions, values, loyalties, and distributions of power and wealth. On the contrary, although we eventually stopped the war, the patterns of social identity that shaped American institutions kept grinding along, and the farther one was from the liberating experience of the movement, the more one resisted and was even enraged by the movement's challenge to the legitimacy of everything that one's conditioning had led one to feel was the basis of one's very social existence and connection to others. Furthermore, the conflict about the very nature of social reality existed within the heart of everyone who was "in" the movement as well as those outside it—we ourselves were threatened by our opposition to the parents who had raised us and whose love and values and ways of life we had internalized, and in any case we had no idea how to create our own new world whole-cloth out of nothing but a powerful, blinding insight when the weight of history had produced the institutions and the means of material subsistence that were the only ways of life that were "really there" in front of us. Thus the "war" that the movement(s) of the 1960s sparked in the culture was a war between two consciousnesses of reality existing not "between" different collections of individuals but side by side within the whole of social consciousness that was still, for the most part (for there were many, many radical experiments that tried to start over from scratch), the inherited world suffused with the norms, ideas, and values of prior generations. Thus the origin of the German radical Rudi Dutschke's famous injunction to all of us who became activists determined to change the world in accordance with our new-found insights: "We've had the sixties. Now for the long march through the institutions."

Legal Education and the Reproduction of Hierarchy is an expression of one ingenious mind's attempt to bring what was authentic in our awareness to an unveiling of the encrusted and "maiming" patterns of passive alienation in one of the institutions that as a totality generated the Vietnam War (55,000 Americans, more than two million Asians dead, for "nothing") and that was trying to continue on indefinitely reproducing this social alienation in future generations. Duncan's book is not mainly about law school, but about the reproduction of hierarchy within the society as a whole in a way that actually constitutes the society by recruiting each new generation to become passive actors, role-players, in relationship to a self-legitimating set of ideas and patterns of deference and authority. It is about law school only in the sense that it is a detailed phenomenological description of one particular such institution that Duncan himself is immersed in and in the sense that his "theory" is precisely that it is through telling the story of his world in enough detail to make it uncontrovertibly recognizable to the reader that one can "recognize" the nature of society as a whole as a consciousness-war more or less corresponding to the big war of the sixties I've just described in larger societal terms. In other words, it is about law school in the very specific sense that law school is training for hierarchy generally, and that law school is one very important hierarchy itself insofar as its training has as its specific aim teaching the "legitimating ideology" that serves to legitimate all of the others. This last point is in fact hardly touched on in this book—it appears only in the description of the role of the curriculum in transmitting the presupposed legitimacy of the basic rules of the "private" capitalist marketplace in contracts, torts, and property during the first year and the center-left consensus of modest reforms of capitalism institutionalized in the New Deal during the second year—but it is a major theme of the rest of most Critical Legal Studies writing, and its minor presence here is an important bridge to that writing. The vast majority of the book in the first six descriptive chapters is devoted to the first main idea of revealing, mainly through the use of concrete expressive examples, how the hierarchy itself reproduces itself as an alienation factory, as a process of bondage.

To understand the book and its relationship to the consciousness-war theory of our society that I am claiming it is an expression of, it is important to grasp that the book was written against the received views of the Left about the role of law and legal education in maintaining the existing order of things. In 1983, the received view prevalent within the National Lawyers Guild and the Left in general was either that law is an instrument of the ruling class, "used" by those in power to maintain their class superiority in relation to an economic system that is the true locus of social struggle, or that law is a potential tool of gradual change through statutory or common-law liberal reforms that will give space to the oppressed to fight for more fundamental change. Duncan spells out his critique of both of these positions in the book itself, mainly by emphasizing, for example, that the market and the State are now so interpenetrated that it is meaningless to say one is "more fundamental" than the other, or that the idea that today's "proletariat" of the marginalized poor (he names welfare mothers, illegal immigrants, and the homeless) is going to lead the revolution is just implausible, or that the reform strategy just can't work because external modifications of the system remain encapsulated within the internal reproduction of hierarchical patterning that is the system. And he shows how both of these theories serve as rationalizations that actually disempower law students from engaging in struggle right now to transform law schools as part of the anarcho-syndicalist, workplace-by-workplace organizing that the book advocates as the cell-by-cell way to actually change the world.

But through the consciousness-war lens of the historical period that I am emphasizing, the most important error in the received Left views of law was precisely that they picture law and legal education as instrumental "tools" of domination within an "entity" called society that actually does not exist—because what does exist is the consciousness-war between authenticity and alienation that is masked and denied precisely by "the reproduction of hierarchy" that keeps spreading itself across the face of the networks of human interaction we call society. Duncan is not denying the existence or importance of economic inequality and injustice or of other forms of inequality and injustice that CLS, as one incarnation of the Left, was/is fighting against. But he is writing a work of expressive revelation that makes a demand on the reader to recognize that the source of the problem is not "out there" but right in front of him or her, a condition of existential servitude to a great nothing (the hierarchy with no heart or center to it) masked by a kind of universal fealty that is just self-deception and "false consciousness." Thus the strategy in the last chapters of the book calls not for changing "society" as if there were some External Thing outside of us that we had to somehow manipulate into democracy and egalitarianism and as lawyers (law professors, law students) "using" law as a "tool" to do so, but rather for cellular organizing to resist the pain right now of having one's existence as a free being "maimed" by a distortion of social consciousness that is always occurring where we are, right now. Within this effort, law is not a "tool" but a part of the consciousness, encoding values legitimating hierarchy that are masked by claims to neutrality and mere craft ("legal reasoning") that can and should be exposed and contested just as the institution, law school, that teaches that law should be.

What is ingenious about the book is not the correctness of this point of view stated abstractly as I have just done, but the revelatory power of the description of law school itself. Every detail of life in law school—from the way the interaction of the hard case and the soft case seduces the student into accepting, and the way each is taught draws the student into believing in, the power of legal as opposed to "non-legal" reasoning; to the way that fatuous attacks on law professors in the law school student paper actually help to constitute the pedestal upon which the very meanest of professors must be located (as does the mercy dispensed by these very professors: "his Clark is worse than his Byse"); to the way that the tiniest of gestures serve as modeling displays made coercive by the fact that everyone watching everyone else follows them (the students seeing "'secretaries' treating 'professors' with elaborate deference, as though her time and her dignity meant nothing and his everything, even when he is not her boss," and that humane relations between them when they occur, "are a matter of the superior's grace, rather than of humane need and social justice"); to the role of law review ("An instant ('the lightening of grades') converts jerks into statesmen; honored spokespeople retire to the margins, shamed"); to the micro-details of social coercion students learn to impose on themselves that both reinforce and erase class and race hierarchies ("Lower-middle class students learn not to wear an undershirt that shows, and that certain patterns and fabrics in clothes will stigmatize them no matter what their grades," while "Black students learn ... that their very presence means affirmative action, unless it means 'he would have made it even without affirmative action'"); to literally a hundred other examples—every detail of law school life is subjected to Duncan's x-ray vision and made transparent as a more or less unified way of life that seems impossible to escape from and serves as training for the later hierarchies of the Bar, whose saints come marching in, as Duncan also describes, beginning with the interview process of the second year and the fancy hotels you will be invited to fly out to stay at and the denial of humiliation that is manifested in the 'ha, ha' mass posting of one's rejection letters in the dorms, and so on and so on and so on right up through one's poignant death (this part is not in the book but is implied by it), when one may realize for the first time that one has lived a life imprisoned in masks that turned into a false self, a life without freedom, authentic personal dignity, and the integrity of self-determination.

As a way of showing both the strengths and limitations of the book as I see it, and of establishing the relation of the book to the work of Critical Legal Studies as a whole, let me again call Duncan's method "expressive revelation" and separate this method into two consciousnesses: Duncan's own consciousness, which I will call the Seeing consciousness, and the consciousness that he is attempting to expressively reveal or unveil, which I will call the Seen consciousness, that of the role-player caught up in the drama of the reproduction of law school hierarchy. In my view, the Seeing consciousness as it is manifested in all of the book's examples of training for hierarchy is brilliantly insightful and is aligned with what I earlier described as the liberating consciousness of the movements of the sixties. The Seeing consciousness purports to be free and is making a powerful appeal to the Seeing consciousness in the reader to identify with this freedom through the unveiling of the false consciousness of the Seen consciousness. And it proposes concrete strategies (cell-by-cell organizing, the Left Study Group) where possibilities of resistance to the enveloping power of the Seen consciousness can be cracked open, resisted, and effectively contested.

So far so good.

But the problem, as I see it, comes with the Seen consciousness, for a central characteristic of the Seen consciousness is that it does not wish to be seen. Indeed, the entire point of the book is to show that this consciousness comes into being through an elaborate process of "imprisonment," in which each act of modeling deference to hierarchy—together producing a kind of unified ubiquity of social interactions, as well as mystifying ideas that cement this hierarchy in the group's self-reflection—is designed both to keep reproducing the hierarchy and to prevent this intention from becoming visible. As Duncan puts it, what is initially a mask becomes the self. His point is precisely that the reproduction of hierarchy is elaborated through what I would call a "circle of collective denial," or through what he on several occasions calls a denial of false consciousness that is coercively made unaware of its own falseness. This aspect of what I am calling the Seen consciousness provides the link between the unveiling insight of the movements of the sixties, its insight into the unreality of a society of people playing roles that are mistaken for "who we really are," and Duncan's own insights into legal education as one important arena where this process takes place and reproduces itself, like an amoeba.

The reason that this aspect of the Seen consciousness is a problem is that the book assumes that the Seen consciousness can be resisted and eventually undone by a spreading of the Seeing consciousness's discovery of its own freedom—through revealing the Seen consciousness for what it is and engaging in forms of political organizing that oppose the hierarchy's false claims in the name of freedom and true collective self-determination. In my view, however, this contradicts the very social nature of the reproduction of hierarchy, in which people gain recognition and their personal identity as social beings connected to others by accommodating to the world of others that surrounds them. Indeed the only plausible explanation for why law students don't spontaneously resist and reject their assimilation to a hierarchy that "maims" them and deprives them of their authentic selfhood is that the reproduction of hierarchy is the reproduction of our own social alienation, to which, absent some liberating social movement that frees us for a more authentic form of social connection, we have no choice but to succumb. To apply this very insight to the revelatory power of the Seeing consciousness, Duncan's own capacity to see through and express the alienated character of legal education and the reproduction of hierarchy generally is not the result of the freedom and insight of a singular individual (here, Duncan himself), but rather the expression of the insight of an era that is itself an expression of an inherently social movement of inherently social beings liberated (only partially, alas) from their social alienation and inherited conditioning by the affirming gaze of the other, with each serving as the other for the other. Just as the coercive denial spread throughout the law school hierarchy is made coercive by making accommodation serve as a condition of social membership and identity, so also the capacity for freedom from the hierarchy—the capacity to even see it as social alienation—requires the other: others who form the more real and more present and more free and more authentically connected consciousness of the movement.

The limitation of Duncan's book is that it does not, in my opinion, accurately analyze the cause of the very "sickness" he describes, a limitation that links the book to what became the dominant point of view in Critical Legal Studies and that must be transcended if we are to pick up where we left off. The work of CLS was always divided into two main strands: what might be called the critique of alienation on the one hand and the neo-legal-realist/deconstruction critique, which became known as the "indeterminacy" critique on the other. In part because of the influence of virtually all of Duncan's other writings about law, the indeterminacy critique became the dominant one within CLS and was devoted almost exclusively to demonstrating in a myriad of specific instances—in hundreds of articles—what is merely alluded to in the first chapter of *Legal Education and the Reproduction of Hierarchy*—namely, that all legal reasoning as well as justifications for the alleged legitimacy of legal reasoning (e.g. the work of Ronald Dworkin) can be shown to be sufficiently vague, circular, self-contradictory, or manipulable so as to not provide any plausible justification claming to legitimately dictate the outcomes of cases. Although in its phenomenological or descriptive aspect, *Legal Education and the Reproduction of Hierarchy* is mainly Duncan's very best published description of the alienation critique, in its separation of the Seeing consciousness and the Seen consciousness the book is also consistent with the indeterminacy critique. For the indeterminacy critique is fundamentally not a critique that uses the social-phenomenological method of "expressive revelation" to unveil the alienated character of legal thought and culture, but is rather what I would call a neo-formalist analytical mode of critique that seeks to affirm the freedom of the reader from the alleged determinacy of legal doctrine and justifications for doctrine. In this respect, the indeterminacy critique spilled into and joined forces with post-structuralism, identity politics, and deconstruction that more or less took over CLS and the academic Left as a whole with the collapse of socialism and Marxist criticism.

The problem with the indeterminacy critique is that it wants to argue for democracy and egalitarianism by showing that we are all free from any purported state of bondage to legal rules and the political justifications for them, but it leaves us each alone in our freedom—it does not want to come to grips with the social nature of the alienation critique, which accounts for the illusion of bondage by its recognition that the Seen consciousness clings to the determinacy and the purported legitimacy of law and legal institutions because it does not wish to become conscious of itself. Whether or not it's a denial of false consciousness, people are just not going to give up their attachment to the alienated networks of passive role-performances, or their belief in the legitimacy of legal reasoning and legal education, if maintaining their allegiance to these modes of alienation is their only apparent source of social identity and self-worth as inherently social beings, that bowing to this alienation is even the seemingly necessary condition of group membership. The relationship of Duncan's book to the indeterminacy critique in CLS scholarship is that both covertly assume that people will want to reclaim their freedom from hierarchy, as well as from the supposed objectivity that rationalizes the legitimacy of legal reasoning, if their freedom from the "false necessity" of following the rules can be shown to them (in the case of hierarchy, through this particular book's method of demystifying "expressive revelation"; in the case of legal reasoning, by the analytical deconstruction of the purported rationality of the thought-process). But this is not the case if freedom's just another word for nothing left to lose, and if un-freedom is the only source of fulfilling the longing for mutual recognition and social connection that inheres in the nature of social existence itself.

It was Martin Luther King who most fully grasped this truth in relation to law when he defined justice as "love correcting that which revolts against love." The point of this idea in relation to the reproduction of hierarchy is that the "sickness" of the "maiming" hierarchies of legal education that Duncan so brilliantly describes is a spiritual sickness that must be healed by new methods of educating lawyers that bind them to the moral ideal of creating a loving and caring society. Like Duncan's book itself, the sixties provided my generation with a glimpse of King's insight, a glimpse of our essential possibility for authentic and loving connection that could transcend the spiritual distortion of our forced allegiance to the legacy of social alienation that we inherited from prior generations and that were indeed, as Duncan says, a form of collective denial of false consciousness. But the glimpse turned out to be too brief and too frightening in its very radicalism to allow us to develop the way out of the claim that our prior conditioning made upon our loyalties; and within both CLS and the sixties themselves, we were not yet able to link the experience of the possibility of liberation-through-each-other with what many spiritual traditions call The Way, the details of the spiritual strategy to successfully transform our servitude to hierarchy into an authentic, beloved community.

What would this mean in relation to the transformation of legal education in a more "just" direction within the meaning of King's definition? Paradoxically, I am in substantial agreement with a core element of the last chapters on "Strategy in Legal Education" and the "Reproduction of Hierarchy"—the vision of an existential, cell-by-cell transformation of the whole in which concrete groups of students, teachers, and lawyers see the hierarchies before them as an unnecessary network of mutually legitimating denial of authentic human longing that rationalizes alienation, domination, and even cruelty and that must be overcome piecemeal, rather than, say, seizing control of the State or the means of production or any of the other "totalizing" strategies that in 1983 were part of the dominant Left fantasy about replacing the current order of things. I also think there is some appropriate and limited value to the indeterminacy critique of legal reasoning as an intellectually helpful part of this process in showing that no political or legal concept, no matter how lofty (liberty, equality, democracy), can be shown to entail a particular result, which is to say, to entail the realization of the ideal claimed by that concept. As one moment of the spiritual awakening that leads our students and ourselves to move toward correcting that which revolts against Love, it is helpful to see that this has nothing to do with the concept of love, which is of course indeterminate in what it entails, but rather with the undistorting, the healing, and the resacralization of our experience of one another as social beings whom we can come to recognize as the source of each other's completion.

But in order to "correct" in King's sense what should have been the main theme of CLS (i.e., that the legal system legitimates social alienation) and what is the main accomplishment of Duncan's book as a critique of legal education as an instance of reproducing social alienation, this path of cellular transformation must be reunderstood as a morally compelling, spiritual activity rather than merely an intellectual/political revolt of free individuals against a surrounding false consciousness. The work of transformation must offer those who engage in it the kind of social healing and legal wisdom that is capable of healing the underlying motivation for the maiming collective denial upon which the book places so much emphasis, a denial that otherwise will not be capable of becoming conscious of itself by overcoming the counter-influence of the processes of social coercion that institutionalize this denial and keep reproducing it, as they have successfully continued to do from 1983 until today.

∗ ∗ ∗

The Project for Integrating Spirituality, Law and Politics, of which I am a member, is a group of lawyers, law teachers, and law students who are trying to do precisely this: to engage in the piecemeal spiritual disalienation and transformation of the legal profession, of which legal education is a very important part. I also work in one cell of legal education, New College of California's public-interest law school, and in a cell within that cell, the first-year course in Contracts that I have taught for almost thirty years.

In that cell within a cell within a cell, every year I teach the case of *O'Neal v. Colton School Board of the State of Washington*. Mr. O'Neal was a long-time school teacher in Colton High School who had developed diabetes and found late one spring that he could no longer read well enough to see his students' papers, read their writing, and read the board in his classroom. During the summer following the end of that year, he reluctantly decided that he had no choice worthy of his students and his school but to inform the School Board that he could not return the following year, although he was under contract to do so. The School Board shocked Mr. O'Neal by replying that he had no justification for "refusing to perform" and rejected his attempted resignation, denying him in the process his request for his accumulated 27-1/2 sick days. The legal issue presented to the students by the casebook and the case itself is whether Mr. O'Neal was excused from "performing" under the doctrine of impossibility of performance.

It is possible to teach this case in many ways. One is to ask a student from a position of superior knowledge, backed by the threat of humiliation and non-recognition of the student's legal talent, a question designed to test the student's capacity to see that Mr. O'Neal should have foreseen the risk of his disabling illness prior to entering his contract and that to excuse him under these circumstances would both undermine personal responsibility for assumed risks and bring inefficiency and instability into market transactions where no transaction costs are present that might justify governmental interference in the market (a law-and-economics method of conditioning students to embrace the legitimacy of competitive individualism and a materialist conception of value popular today, although largely unheard of in 1983). Another certainly more common approach would be to use the same interpersonal methods to compare Mr. O'Neal's resignation to, say, a deep-sea diver's refusal to go through with an agreement to dive for valuable pearls for fear of being attacked by sharks, an exercise in distinguishing cases involving foreseeable risks that eliminates the fancy philosophy (if law-and-economics can be considered such) and reduces legal reasoning to more of a trade involving cleverness but transmitting the same values to students. Still a third, more liberal approach would be to adopt the same superior stance as the teacher but treat *O'Neal v. Colton* as just an easy case to get across the rule that serious illness forms the basis for a valid impossibility defense in employment cases, but focus on the Court's formalistic refusal to allow him the sick days, which the Court in fact says fell through because accumulated sick days must be claimed before the end of one's employment, and the contract was terminated at the moment of impossibility when the diabetes disabled Mr. O'Neal from performing. Even more "political" would be an effort to bring out the labor movement's long struggle to win the granting of accumulated sick days at all for workers in a market characterized by inequality of wealth and power and the injustice of the opinion's formalism in light of the length of Mr. O'Neal's employment.

Personally, in my cell, I have used all of the foregoing methods, although to the extent that I employ the "Socratic" posture in my egalitarian school, I do it playfully, to remove the (in my opinion) absurd implication that it is humiliating not to know the fancy (1) or clever (2) or historically informed (3) answer. And I explicitly bring out at the end of this portion of the discussion what the rule is in employment cases.

But then I ask a question that addresses what I honestly deeply feel about Mr. O'Neal as I have thought about him and his family over the years. I ask a student how a local community ought to respond with justice to a long-time, perhaps venerated high school teacher who has taught most if not all the children in the town of Colton, many of whom are now grown, many of whom now have children of their own who benefited from Mr. O'Neal's teaching. Under all of the traditional approaches to teaching the case described above, the very best treatment Mr. O'Neal receives means going home alone with a little money to at most his wife and children, if he has a wife and children, to rattle around in retirement half-blind until he dies. Might it be our legal obligation—that is, the legal obligation of the School Board as the embodiment of the community—to keep him on as an elder, to make sure he is venerated and appreciated and taken care of and even given an active mentoring role in the school that doesn't require the eyesight acuity of everyday teaching? Mightn't this elevate the later years of Mr. O'Neal's life, give great pleasure to his former students, bring a greater sense of community to the high school as a whole, and strengthen the high school's ties to the rest of the town?

In my view, it is this sort of approach, writ large and reimagined toward transforming the whole moral and spiritual nature of the curriculum as well as informing the teaching of the very nature of the social interventions one might consider trying to make as a lawyer in the school's clinics and later as a lawyer in practice, that undermines the reproduction of hierarchy and carries forward the promise of Critical Legal Studies. The reason is that this approach touches on the longing for a beloved community, and of law as a path to the creation of such a community, that exists in each of us—indeed even consciously in virtually all law students on the first day of law school before they are conditioned to become clever, cynical arguers for the materialist self-interest of clients at the expense of their brothers and sisters. Or to put it differently, in my view there is no "opposite" of the reproduction of social alienation and hierarchy except for the experience of love and community, and then the reproduction of the experience until it becomes confident of itself. As Duncan's dear and lifelong friend, I actually am confident that this is the inspiration behind his "Polemic Against the System"—his brilliant and, at the time of publication, daring little red book.

ESSAY THREE

CRITICAL LEGAL STUDIES AS A SPIRITUAL PRACTICE

I

I ASSUME THAT I WAS ASKED TO SPEAK on a panel entitled "The Higher Law and Its Critics" because the organizers of this conference believed that as a Critical Legal Studies (CLS) founder and writer, I'd debunk the idea that there is any higher law. They likely felt that CLS stands for the idea that law and the interpretations of law are just an expression of social power, and that any claim that there exists a higher law which the existing legal world somehow exists in relation to would just be regarded by CLS as a form of ideology—mystifying, masking, and rationalizing existing power relations in society.

So let me start by saying that while appeals to a Higher Law certainly can be used to rationalize unjust power relations, I do not at all believe that they must do so; and even more, that I believe CLS was always fundamentally a spiritual enterprise that sought to liberate law and legal interpretation from its self-referential, circular, and ideological shackles. The CLS movement, after all, emerged in response to the moral intensity of the broader social movements of the 1960s, and was an attempt to join forces with the civil rights movement, the anti-war movement, the women's and workers' movements to challenge the status quo on behalf of a higher moral vision of what human relations could be like—a vision of a world in which people treated each other with true equality and respect and affection and kindness, and in which people saw each other as fully human and beautiful, rather than as cogs in a machine or as self-interested monads out for their own gain or as any of the other ways of characterizing human beings that seemed to be commonplace within the system as it was. In CLS, we were against the inhumanity of the system as it really was and as it really functioned, and we were against the existing legal system to the extent that it sought, consciously or unconsciously, to rationalize the inhumanity of the existing social world and call it something good, the embodiment of liberty and equality.

Thus there was always a spiritual impulse behind the work and the politics of CLS. But it is absolutely the case that CLS—or at least what came to be known as the dominant strain within CLS—refused to embrace this transcendent spiritual impulse, to stand behind it, or to speak about it. We really were motivated by love, but it was a love that dared not speak its name. And in my opinion, that is because our movement was infected with the same fear of the other that underlay the injustices that we criticized in the wider society. We were motivated by a powerful moral transcendent impulse that was an expression of what this conference is calling a Higher Law, but we would not say so, or to be honest, some of us would not say so. On this point, there was a division inside CLS, and in my opinion the wrong side carried the day—but today is another day.

The view that won out inside CLS is what became known as the indeterminacy critique—the idea that legal principles are so abstract and indefinite that they can be used to rationalize virtually any outcome. The literature of CLS has produced hundreds of articles demonstrating this point,[1] but an excellent example not cited so far as I know in existing CLS writing is the legal opinions produced during the rise of the Nazi movement in Germany, in which conventional liberal legal doctrines were reinterpreted by the judiciary to be made consistent with the ideology of the ascendant Nazi party. Thus the German equivalent of the doctrine of "good faith" in landlord-tenant contracts was interpreted not to prevent the otherwise illegal eviction of Jews because Jews were threats to the German people.[2] Using the indeterminacy critique, CLS writers showed in article after article that just as the eviction of Jews could be made consistent with contractual good faith, virtually any legal argument could be made consistent, via the open-ended nature of legal interpretation, with virtually any legal outcome. That being so, the actual explanation of legal outcomes must come from outside of legal reasoning itself—from the realm of politics or conviction or commitment to particular values on the part of the person or group doing the interpreting. And wonderful CLS writers like Duncan Kennedy, Mark Tushnet, Gary Peller, or Betty Mensch[3]—who contributed to this discussion at the Higher Law Symposium—showed that it was no answer to this critique to find some other supposed "anchor" for legal reasoning in the political or moral principles of the wider society that would shape the legal thought-process, for these political and moral principles could always be shown to be just as abstract and indefinite in their concrete meaning in any particular case and therefore just as indeterminate in their application.

There was much to be said for the indeterminacy critique as an analytical technique that could help a new generation of legal intellectuals and law students to challenge the authority of received justifications for the status quo, especially the authority of those who claimed that things had to be the way they were in late twentieth century capitalist society because the rule of law required it to be so. Many a law student who had come to law school with a longing to contribute to the creation of a more humane and just world had been subtly talked out of their idealism by sophisticated law professors who were better at manipulating concepts than they were and could use the power relations of the law school classroom to make their instinctive idealism appear naïve or childish or dumb. Armed with the indeterminacy critique and backed by the solidarity of other writers, teachers, and students who shared their transformative aspirations, these same students could better stand up for themselves and demonstrate that their professors' pretensions to superiority of reasoning amounted to no more than a preference for the existing system. Certainly a fifty-page opinion by Justice Scalia in his black robes is far less humbling to the radical spirit if one can show that all of its weighty argumentation and compilation of precedential authority amount to no more than a statement by the writer than "I like capitalism."

But there was a major problem with the indeterminacy critique—namely, that it was a headless horseman, an analytical method without moral content that could not itself point the practitioner in any moral direction. Like all analytical critiques that rely upon logic to challenge claims to conceptual rationality, the indeterminacy critique is indifferent to the meaning of its object—it employs its scalpel at a distance from whatever may be morally compelling about a claim and satisfies itself with the assertion that a claim purporting to be logically valid is actually not so.

This creates three problems that, in my view, are decisive. First, the logical indeterminacy of abstract concepts, legal or otherwise, does not take account of the power of the moral environment in which such concepts exercise social force. To the extent that human beings are inherently moral beings animated by the longing for meaning and the desire to live in a better, more morally resonant world, the power of law and legal concepts will depend upon the social forces that give weight to a particular moral vision and related moral ideas at particular historical moments. If a particular worldview gains sway by virtue of its socially-anchored moral resonance, then the legal arguments that follow from that worldview will be heard and understood as logical to those who embrace the moral dimension of the worldview whether or not the arguments are logically compelled in the abstract. The Supreme Court's decision in *Bush v. Gore* deciding the 2000 presidential election seemed to many scholars to validate the indeterminacy critique[4] because the Court's reasoning to the result it wanted seemed to almost randomly change between its first decision (based on Article II's reservation of power to the State legislatures to choose electors to the Electoral College),[5] and the second final decision terminating the Florida vote-count on the grounds of the Equal

Protection Clause.[6] In addition, the final decision seemed to contradict the Court's new-federalist deference in other opinions to a state's right to manage its own elections within broad parameters that should have included the then-unfolding Florida recount.[7] But as I show in *What it Really Means to Say "Law is Politics": The Political Meaning of Bush v. Gore*[8] [see Essay Five, p. 71], the significant fact is that the decision was found acceptable by Gore and his constituencies in spite of all the grumbling because of historical factors—including the rise of Ronald Reagan, thirty years of conservative ascendancy in political and legal thought, and the collapse of the Soviet Union and parallel collapse of any worldwide public sphere in which morally compelling democratic social movements could challenge conventionally legitimated democratic institutions—that made the Supreme Court's decision plausible enough to the moral self-understanding of the then-existing national constituency.[9] Reduced to a sentence, this is to say that the indeterminacy critique, because of its very abstraction and disconnection from immanent meaning, cannot reach what is morally compelling about a legal argument and, therefore, cannot negate the argument to a really existing historical listener anchored in a web of real social relations.

The second problem with the amoral nature of the indeterminacy critique is that to the extent that human beings are moral beings decisively animated by the longing for meaning, purpose, and a better world, the indeterminacy critique cannot convey a moral vision of how we are to create such a world and therefore cannot gain any true adherents. In other words, the indeterminacy critique is basically a bummer, leaving the listener in a kind of secular liberal hell of scattered and disconnected individuals with no common passion or direction binding us together. Not only did this erasure of moral purpose disarm the CLS movement of its most compelling spiritual feature—namely its link to a powerful, transformative vision of a socially just world—it also seemed to dismiss as unimportant, and even trivial and misguided, the experience of moral dislocation, social isolation, and meaninglessness that is precisely the most spiritually painful aspect of modern liberal culture. While a few writers tried to justify CLS's "nihilism" as a bracing affirmation of freedom, emphasizing that the critique was only a critique of the authority of reason and not of strongly held, freely affirmed values,[10] this defense simply cast the listener back into the spiritual void of his/her liberal solitude rather than purposefully pointing the listener forward toward the moral world that would finally connect us.

The third and final problem with the valorization of the indeterminacy critique and its preeminence within the CLS movement is that it could be and was used against the movement's own spiritual commitments. Although conservatives were fond of caricaturing CLS writers as a group of radical cynics who didn't believe in anything,[11] most were just the opposite—wonderful, loving, caring people committed to helping others and changing the world in accordance with a moral devotion to mutual affirmation and social equality. But the indeterminacy critique prohibited them from saying so in a universal, visionary language because any such discourse was itself indeterminate, and could be stolen away by the other and used to rationalize domination. Backed up by Derrida's in-fashion critique of "phallologocentrism"[12]—the historical tendency of abstract male-dominated ideologies to marginalize and dismiss the insights of minority cultures—some CLS writers would just make fun of those of us whose critique of law and legal culture was rooted in a substantive, moral vision of community and equality, as if we failed to grasp that the same critique we ourselves had embraced—the use of abstract universals to legitimize the injustices of liberal society—could be used against ourselves. Did we not see that the devil can cite scripture for his/her purpose and that any universal ideal with which we purported to ground our critique of law could be used to justify the opposite of the meaning we sought to give it? How did we think that an ideal of spiritual community could be the "basis" of anything at all, since it could as easily entail a society of crystal-gazers or religious fundamentalists as it could the loving and egalitarian world to which we aspired?

It is worth pausing for a moment on this last point because it contains an epistemological confusion—or at least a difference of opinion and orienting attitude toward knowledge—that establishes the groundwork for my turn to a discussion of the existence of a higher law and a turn to what could give meaning to a rebirth of critical legal studies as the spiritual practice that I am claiming it always was.

When the practitioner of the indeterminacy critique rejects the idea that an abstraction like "spiritual community" can be the "basis" of a critique of the status quo, citing the indeterminacy of the meaning of the abstraction, he or she is thinking within the analytical epistemology embedded in the indeterminacy critique itself—as if the relationship of the abstraction to the concrete manifestation, or the universal to the particular, is a relationship of logical entailment of a concept. Thus from this point of view, the critique of the liberal ideals of freedom and equality that are embedded in all of American law is that their very abstract and universal nature can be manipulated in a way that allows the concrete meaning of these ideals to legitimize the unfreedom and inequality of free market capitalism. The critique is that in liberal society, freedom equals free competition and equality means equality to compete in a universal marketplace that actually reproduces, in real life, the inequalities of class society and the unfreedom of servitude to hierarchy. From this truth (and other analogous ones that can be drawn from the concrete histories of pre-liberal societies, from socialism as actualized in socialist societies, and so on across and throughout history), the indeterminacy practitioner concludes that all abstract universals are similarly manipulable and subject to the same logical abuses in the service of legitimation. Because the indeterminacy critique begins and ends in an attitude of moral detachment from its object and analyzes the unfolding of the object through its merely possible logical expressions, the critique rejects a priori (in other words, as a matter of "belief" and not on the basis of its own critique!) that there could be moral "essence" to the object that gives moral direction to the critique of, say, the liberal conceptions of freedom and equality.

The paradox here is evident and refers back to my initial comments: for CLS is and was animated by a vision of overcoming the inhumanity and injustice of the world, and not by mere analytical cleverness or skill at deconstructing concepts. Caught in the epistemological straight-jacket of their own making, the proponents of the indeterminacy critique managed to make themselves unable to offer any "basis" for their own passionately held moral starting point, declaring that these motivating convictions were "irrational" and outside the realm of rational knowledge, like the relationship of chaos theory to normal science.[13] Far from being a bad thing, these CLSers believed that this irrationalism would protect the critical aspect of critical legal studies from absorption into falsifying rationalistic ideologies and maintain a liberated free-space for political action in support of their irrationalist convictions. The politics of this position was then that there should and could be a public, democratic debate among competing convictions—left, right, and center—about what kind of social world and what kind of legal culture we humans should be aspiring to create, a debate unburdened by any transcendent moral claims which appeal to a non-existent, or at least unknowable, transcendent moral authority whose very investiture with social power would reproduce our subordination to some Other that would not be ourselves.

Unfortunately, the validity of this view rested on a "belief" about the very nature of social reality that is, with all due respect to my long-time comrades who hold it, wrong. For the world as it really is is suffused with moral longing that pulls upon the conscience of humanity to elevate ourselves from the limitations of what is toward the realization of what ought to be, and the evocation of precisely that longing has been the decisive force behind every social movement that has advanced the development of humanity toward a loving and humane common existence since the beginning of time. It is equally true that the appeal to this moral longing has been the basis for terrible injustice and suffering. But this struggle over the way forward is a moral struggle anchored in the capacity of every one of us to manifest ourselves to each other in a way that points us in the right direction. A successful critical approach to the present—or in the case of law, to a successful critical legal studies—requires the illumination of the injustice of what is that is anchored in a transcendent intuition of the just world that ought to be.

II

During Friday night Shabbat services at my synagogue Beyt Tikkun in San Francisco (Beyt Tikkun means House of Healing and Repairing), we always go outside in a whirl of dancing, holding hands in long lines, and singing "Tov Le'Hodot La'Adonai" ("It's Good to Give Thanks to G-d"). By this time, our rabbi has already stipulated that the God we do not believe in does not exist so that we do not have to spend our time worrying about it, and our goal is to elevate our awareness, to apprehend the miraculous nature of the universe as we turn away, at "sundown," from the mysterious great ball of fire one million times larger than our own planet and face the other billions of fireballs in what we call the sky. To apprehend this magnificence while singing and dancing with other whirling comrades is just... Wow! ... as the prayers say. It takes you out of the humdrum flatness of everyday existence, in which this same earth and sky appear as mere objects before us as we carry out our functional activities, in which our minds are racing from thought to thought distracting us from Being Present, or better yet, in the words of Ram Das, from Being Here. Even more, the whirl of the spiral dance allows us to make eye contact with each other, to actually see each other as radiant spiritual beings, with open hearts and bursting with recognition as we share this amazing experience of where we actually are, where we have actually been all day. How remarkably different this collective encounter is from the reciprocal withdrawnness, from the mutual solitude of the day, as we woke up, got out of bed, dragged a comb across our heads, found our way downstairs and drank a cup, and somebody spoke and we went into a dream....[14]

The very purpose of this spiritual practice is to bring ourselves into contact with the world behind the world, by lifting our spirit to deepen our awareness of the phenomena before us so as to unveil a spiritual and moral meaning that is obscured by the leveled-down empirical perception of everyday life. The poet William Blake brilliantly captured the necessity of this deepening of awareness for gaining access to truth when he said, "We are led to Believe a Lie When we see [with], not Thro', the Eye."[15] And it is just this kind of access to another dimension of reality that is sometimes made possible by social movements, in which people emerge from the passive station of their reciprocal isolation into a new kind of connection, a new "mutual recognition," that allows the seemingly fixed appearance of the world to dissolve, revealing a spiritual depth that had previously been "unconscious" in the sense of inaccessible to conscious knowledge.[16] Historical moments touched by these movements often produce outpourings of intellectual and cultural creativity, as people in disparate locations begin to express the new insight in a burst of music, literature, intellectual work, and activism, all of it seeking to "realize" what we've been given an intimation of. And the work that is thus produced can have the effect of altering the entire social landscape to such a degree that no one is free not to admit some relation to what is going on, not to "admit that the waters around you have grown,"[17] to swim, or to refuse to swim and try to get the waters to go down.

The 1960s was certainly such a period, and I suspect that forty years later many of us in this room are still trying to establish our relationship to the breakthrough of consciousness that altered our way of seeing the world itself and the meaning of our existence within it as we ourselves constitute it. By way of analogy to my description of the elevation of consciousness during the Shabbat service at my synagogue, the sixties should be understood as a dawning of awareness that unfolded through the overlapping influence of the civil rights movement's illumination of injustice, the evocative power of Martin Luther King, Jr., the linguistic fissures and image-scrambles produced by the Beat poets, the song, dance, and creative movement of rock n' roll, the youthful moral eloquence of JFK, and the consequent emergence of a student movement, a women's movement, a gay liberation and sexual liberation movement, and an environmental movement that expressed an opening up of the heart allowing a new kind of sight into what we came to see as the insanity of the fixed and rigid posture and thinking that was producing the Vietnam war, with its 55,000 American and more than two million Asian dead.[18]

Within the critical legal studies movement that was itself an expression of this upsurge in awareness, we were confronted by a "legal order" and hierarchical institutions that supported this order that seemed to allow no room whatsoever for the sense of love, hope, and transcendence that we felt ineffably all around us. On the contrary, it seemed to be an enormous, spiritually dead thought-machine that produced and reproduced both hierarchies and rules that made the world of the war, and racial hatred, and sexual repression, and environmental destruction appear entirely normal and inevitable. And this disjunction between our dawning, idealistic awareness and the professional settings in which we found ourselves as young adults led us to throw ourselves into trying to (a) take apart the fixity of, and (b) reveal the meaning of what everywhere surrounded us.

Here we come to the key split that developed within CLS. The part of the work that was motivated by "taking apart the fixity" of the legal order became the indeterminacy critique, and the part that was motivated by "revealing the meaning" of that order became the critique of alienation, to which I shall now turn. Located within this historical process, it is clear, I hope, that the work of these two strands within CLS was at first complementary, in the sense that both were intended to be in service of a breakthrough to another level of social being and knowledge in which our idealistic vision of a more loving and caring world would become possible. That they became separated was too bad, the result of the effects of fear and loss of confidence in our transcendent hopes as we were complexly enveloped by the rise of Ronald Reagan, by tenure struggles, and related dilemmas of personal identity as we ebbed away from each other with the ebbing of the sixties themselves, and by the resulting defensiveness and separation within our own groups. But for reasons that I will return to, we are now approaching a new historical moment in which a reunification of our efforts may become possible.

In the case of both the Shabbat service consciousness and the social movement consciousness, a transformation of our social being takes place that allows a transformation of our knowledge of the world. In each case, prior to the transformation, we exist underneath the weight of our inherited conditioning, cemented within our pre-existing social roles, eyes darting away from each other's gaze, withdrawn into our separateness and seeing the world from a detached state, a solitude which we assume to be natural, the way things are. Without realizing it, we exist in a state of secret fear of the other, preoccupied unconsciously with keeping the other at a distance, and in a state of denial of the world's loving and transformative energy.[19] We try to close ourselves up, and to treat the world around us as equally closed or fixed, because we are afraid to reveal what has not been confirmed. But through the outbreak of connection permitted by the singing and dancing and expressive discourse of the service and movement, we attain a new level of mutual recognition which in turn confirms a new kind of insight into the "fallen" and despiritualized nature of the world. From a philosophical / epistemological point of view, a change in both the subject and object occurs, such that the being of the knower finds a new moral platform with which to see the world as suffering under the weight of its own alienation and separation, and the being of the known object or "world" becomes suddenly transparent in its depth-dimension as something not fixed according to its prior surface appearance, but as alienated and in need of a restorative salvation. Or to put this in yet another way: The recovery of each of us as subjects through the spiritual elevation of mutual recognition provides the inter-subjective ground that reveals the moral deficit in the world as object-of-knowledge. Martin Luther King Jr. made exactly this point when he defined justice as "love correcting that which revolts against love."[20]

Thus the type of insight that emerges from the ratcheting up of awareness allowed by the upsurge of confirmatory recognition is an inherently spiritual and moral awareness that both critiques the falsity of what is as an alienated appearance trying to deny its own falsity, and at the same instant points in a moral direction toward bringing into being a world that embodies the connection that has allowed our confirmatory recognition to take place.[21] Why would we want to kill the Viet Cong? They are not "them," they are us, G-d's children, and furthermore, we are not the "fellow Americans" that Lyndon Johnson keeps referring to, but vessels of universal humanity scattered apart in an historical shatter that must be repaired.[22] As we elevate our awareness by uplifting each other through a new mutual recognition, fixed nationalities appear as imaginary, as collective defense mechanisms born of an entire world of mutual fear, and in need of a compassionate spiritual redemption so that we as "peoples" might appear to ourselves not as alien threats to each other, but as unique incarnations of a common humanity.

To the strand of CLS that emerged from this kind of insight, the problem with law was not that it was indeterminate and therefore a mask for political choices made by free individuals, but that it was serving as a legitimating vehicle for our alienation from one another, making our alienation appear to be the embodiment of justice and obscuring our true spiritual and moral destiny as communal beings, a destiny that we had glimpsed through the redemptive insights of our participation in the movement. In reality, it was this "alienation critique" that was the entire basis for the CLS critique of law as legitimating ideology, because the critique necessarily refers to a transcendent moral horizon to challenge the ideology's claims to legitimacy. For as I have already said, insofar as an aspect of legal ideology is "believed in" as a moral discourse supporting the status quo, it cannot be dismissed by a showing of its logical indeterminacy, but only by revealing, through our anchorage in a transcendent moral vantage point, the "determinate" meaning of the legal ideology as an act of legitimation, as a kind of advertisement for a morally impoverished state of affairs.

This then is the true relationship between CLS and what this conference is calling a "Higher Law"—a higher law not as a metaphysical or religious abstraction, but as an embodiment of the presence of social justice manifesting itself in the real world through a spiritually elevating movement that provides a moral horizon for revealing what must be changed about the world, in part through the progressive transformation of legal culture, through law.

Here are eight examples from CLS that appeal to a higher law so defined:

- Karl Klare's critique of the Supreme Court's use of a new post-New Deal ideology of "social conceptualism" to steal away the democratic aspirations of working people as they expressed themselves through the upsurge of the labor movement (*Judicial Deradicalization of the Wagner Act and the Origins of Modern Legal Consciousness, 1937-1941*).[23]

• Alan Freeman's critique of the Supreme Court's use of an individualistic conception of racial discrimination as bad acts by isolated "perpetrators" as a way of naturalizing and legitimizing the ongoing societal racism suffered by its victims (*Legitimizing Racial Discrimination Through Antidiscrimination Law*).[24]

• Duncan Kennedy's demonstration of how Blackstone's Commentaries absorbed and transformed the legal statuses of feudal hierarchies (from The Law of Wrongs to Incorporeal Hereditaments) to rationalize the emerging bourgeois hierarchies of pre-liberal societies in the eighteenth century (*The Structure of Blackstone's Commentaries*).[25]

• Paul Harris's and my account of how the architecture of courtrooms induce deference to the legitimacy of legal hierarchies in a way that confers political legitimacy on social and economic institutions that claim to be expressions of popular will, but are actually expressions of social alienation (*Building Power and Breaking Images: Critical Legal Theory and the Practice of Law*).[26]

• Mary Joe Frug's critique of the legitimation of male toughness in common law contract doctrine from the vantage point of women who care about the welfare of their contracting partners (*Re-reading Contracts: A Feminist Analysis of a Contracts Casebook*).[27]

• Anthony Cook's articulation of the importance of experientially-based insight, growing out of religious practice and social struggle, to the reconstruction of just communities (*Beyond Critical Legal Studies: The Reconstructive Theology of Dr. Martin Luther King, Jr.*).[28]

• William Forbath's analysis of how the American labor movement's moral vision of an egalitarian society rooted in mutuality and solidarity was constrained and reshaped by workers' encounter with the individualist categories of American law (*Law and the Shaping of the American Labor Movement*).[29]

• Rhonda Magee Andrews's argument that the realization of equality within the meaning of the Fourteenth Amendment requires legal recognition of the existential suffering and denial of humanity produced by racial subordination and the creation of remedies based on a substantive vision of human dignity (*Racial Suffering as Human Suffering: An Existentially-Grounded Humanity Consciousness as a Guide to a Fourteenth Amendment Reborn*).[30]

None of these works makes use of the indeterminacy critique, and all of them are moral statements in which existing (or then-existing) legal regimes obscured or deflected the struggle for a more humane and just world.

III

In my view, CLS "stopped," or perhaps "paused," about fifteen years ago because it lost track of this spiritual and moral foundation. One reason for this was the dissipation of the social movements of the sixties themselves, which undermined the intuitive social ground of confirmatory recognition which made this spiritual dimension visible to CLS teachers and writers and audible to our listeners and readers. A second reason influencing the dissipation of the movements themselves was the collapse of socialism and the Marxism that had supported it, which for 150 years provided the principal metaphor for the morally transcendent communal horizon against which the shortcomings of the present society had been measured. A third factor intimately bound up with the other two was the rise of the New Right as a conservative moral response to the social challenge and disruption that the movements of the sixties had introduced into public space, with the Reagan Revolution championing deregulation, an attack on entitlement programs, and an originalist, new-federalist constitutionalism that sought to delegitimate the public sphere itself as an arena of collective moral action. Faced with this loss of footing at both the experiential and ideological levels (or at the levels of both intuitive understanding and reflective interpretation), we lost confidence in the forward trajectory that had united us. Deprived of an anchor-point in the future that could unite our project in the present, we tumbled back into the social separation of the wider system—our professional "roles" congealed around us and our social identities were reabsorbed by the hierarchical institutions we had hoped to transform.

The ascendancy of the indeterminacy critique and its separation from the spiritual and moral foundation within which it was originally located was an expression of this social and moral hemorrhage, as CLS became increasingly identified with a specialized analytical technique of doctrinal deconstruction that could be assimilated by the academy as merely a school of legal thought. And robbed of its morally compelling message, CLS has proved no match for the Law and Economics movement as its principal competitor to be the successor to the normative paradigms of the New Deal (Legal Realism and the Legal Process School); for the Law and Economics movement is rooted in the moral ideal of the market as the social realization of individual liberty and popular democracy. Indeed, at the ontological/epistemological level, it is difficult to distinguish the CLS of the indeterminacy critique from the Law and Economics movement because they both presuppose that free of illegitimate constraints, the world is a free competition (or a "democracy of interpretations") among the free choices (or ideas/convictions) of individual actors, with the CLS critique of the authority of abstraction and any socially binding universal vision being the analogue to the Law and Economics critique of Big Government. Neither point of view apprehends the world as an intersubjective life-world with an intelligible social essence that can be the basis for moral insight and transformative social action.

But it's not too late! For the way out for CLS is to return to its original instincts as a righteous social transformation movement and this time recognize that there is a spiritual basis for our understanding of the social individual that is rooted not in the materialism of Marxism or state socialism, but in the enlivening mutual recognition, or Love, that was always at the heart of the movement out of which CLS was born. Human beings are bound together not primarily by their relationship to the means of production or any other shaping practical medium, but by the desire for confirmation within a loving community that will have overcome the legacy of alienation and social separation. The work of CLS is both to illuminate how that legacy has created a legal culture that has legitimized this alienation by making it seem natural and just, and by beginning to construct a new legal culture that would strengthen and help to realize the loving bond between us: the bond that actually unites us as social beings.

This calls not for a rejection of past CLS work, but for a reclaiming of the spiritual dimension of that work. And this in turn requires a re-understanding of the indeterminacy critique as being merely an analytical moment within the synthesis of a moral critique, as a kind of analytical insight that indicates that the world is open-textured but not going nowhere, and that legal reasoning's claims that would fix the world in idealized, reified abstractions legitimizing injustice and alienation are actually a passivizing defense against the freedom and creative challenge of social vulnerability and uncharted possibility.

But this also requires a new agenda for our movement that cooperates with the world-wide spiritual-political initiatives that have sprung up since the post-sixties era from which CLS first emerged, and that would be tremendously supportive of our efforts. These spiritual-political initiatives include the religious renewal movements that are linking the spiritual ideal of the beloved community to social action and social change; spiritually informed secular movements like the Network of Spiritual Progressives that are trying to invent new forms of spiritual activism while rethinking foreign and domestic social policy reforms to emphasize spiritual transformation rather than merely liberal redistribution of resources and rights;[31] and the efforts of the environmental and ecology movements to link the redemption of the planet with social healing and sustainable, cooperative economies.

All of these efforts require a new legal culture that links justice with explicitly spiritual outcomes—outcomes that foster empathy, compassion, and social connection rather than the vindication of liberal rights in a legal order founded upon the fear-based separation of self and other. One lesson that CLS scholarship itself has taught is that it is impossible for a social transformation movement to be successful without an ability to express its own ideals as also ideals of justice that can achieve legitimate political expression through legal culture. Without that, as Karl Klare, Alan Freeman, and many others have shown,[32] the movement's radical ideals will be recast and stolen away by the liberal interpretations those movements will suffer through the prism of legal assumptions that actually contradict them. Thus while the movement must create the "parallel universe" that can affirm the ontological/epistemological validity of the possibility of a society based on love and mutual recognition, the movement also requires a legal expression of itself that declares this same realization of love and mutual recognition to be indispensable to just outcomes of social conflicts.

Such a parallel justice system has already begun to sprout up across the legal landscape, alongside the antagonism of self and other presupposed and reinforced by the mainstream's adversary system. Among its manifestations are the truly remarkable Restorative Justice movement, which understands crime and social violence as expressive of a breakdown in community and aspires to apology and forgiveness through direct encounters between victims and offenders as a means of restoration of the communal fabric;[33] the transformative and understanding-based mediation movements that make compassion a central objective to the resolution of civil conflicts;[34] the new forms of spiritually-informed law practice that are redefining the lawyer-client relationship as a non-technical, holistic relationship in which lawyers bring a substantive moral and healing vision to bear on the client's perception of his or her "interests" and the relation of those interests to the well-being of the larger community;[35] and the transformation of legal education away from a focus on the mere manipulation of existing rules and doctrine, toward a more humane and spiritually integrated conception of law and justice.

What these new efforts need from a revitalized critical legal studies movement is a scholarship and pedagogy that provides in every field a critique of existing law and legal culture that reveals the limitations of the liberal worldview out of which the existing order was constructed in the centuries since the Enlightenment, and that points toward the socially connected community that ought to be its successor. It is this intellectual piece of the puzzle that is lacking from all of the recent efforts to transform legal practice in the ways I have just described; all of these efforts without exception, as far as I know, challenge the individualized, antagonistic, and despiritualized character of the adversary system without challenging the substantive content of existing law or the analytical thought process of legal reasoning. Both of these elements of legal culture—the critique of the substance of legal rules and doctrine, and the critique of detached, analytical rule-application through abstract, logical technique resting on a normative foundation—require a cadre of intellectuals to help disassemble what is and point to what ought to be, as a "moment" in the transformation from the individualistic, liberal world we inhabit to a post-liberal socially connected, loving, and compassionate world to which we aspire.

So, for example, a CLS course in Contracts should subordinate its use of the indeterminacy critique to a meaning-centered critique emphasizing how the rules presupposing the legitimacy and desirability of individualistic, self-interested bargains (adjusted by a touch of concern for "the reliance interest") among an infinite number of socially disconnected strangers bound by no common moral purpose or spiritually bonded social community outside their respective blood relatives are rapidly destroying the planet, in part, by making use of liberal abstractions like freedom of choice that make it appear that this lonely destiny is what people really want. Or a course in Torts should make it clear to students that there is more to the obligations born of our essential connection to each other as social beings than the duty to not pull chairs out from under each other as we are about to sit down to dinner, or not to smash into each others' cars, or injure each other with exploding Coke bottles—that the bond of recognition itself, and what Emmanuel Levinas calls the ethical demand of the face of the other,[36] means we have a duty to rescue each other, that we must take care of each other, including the poor, the homeless, and those who lack health care.

CLS scholars and teachers should extend—and in many instances already have extended—this kind of critical analysis to every area of law, including developing a critical reflection on the Constitution as a liberal and individualistic document that was a great advance in its time but now must be transformed to embrace a newly evolving vision of spiritual community that was not even conceived of as a universal necessity in the late eighteenth century when it was drafted. Concomitant with the transformation of doctrine must come a transformation of remedy, beyond money damages passed between socially separated litigants conceived as interested only in material outcomes, and beyond a due process model of civil and criminal procedure that links justice to merely the vindication of rights through the dutiful monitoring of a fact-based public hearing that leaves the parties as disconnected or more disconnected than when their legal process began. And finally, supporting such a re-visioning of doctrine, remedy, and process must be a rethinking of legal reasoning itself that goes beyond the normative circularity of the application of indeterminate rules presupposing the legitimacy of the secular liberal order toward a morally grounded reflection anchored in the common effort to realize the values of love, compassion, and mutual concern and well-being that are being carried forward by the movement itself as it tries to link the transformative element of its own social being with a new legal knowledge that would be expressive of it.

If CLS would embrace the moral and spiritual agenda that I'm proposing here, it would instantly revitalize itself. Everywhere today there are law students and young legal scholars trying to figure out how to devote their lives and work to addressing the problems of global warming and the destruction of the environment, to overcoming the social violence and irrationality of religious fundamentalism and pathological, secular nationalism, and to challenging the human indifference of corporate globalization and its blind and reeling world markets. But Marxist materialism can no longer speak to these new generations of potential activists who have become aware that these problems require a spiritually grounded solution, and after a thirty-year assault by the New Right, no one believes any longer in the model of regulatory government as morally capable of containing and altering a civil society founded upon fear of the other and private self-interest. A new spiritual activism actually connecting self and other is clearly what is needed, and it is already coming into being in hundreds of hopeful incarnations. If CLS were to rediscover itself as the legal-intellectual expression of that worldwide effort, it could once again challenge legal education and legal scholarship to become vehicles of the creation of a better world, connecting the worthwhile body of work already produced by its older generations with new, more spiritually confident work yet to be written by the young.

CHAPTER NOTES

[1] *See, e.g.,* Duncan Kennedy, A Critique of Adjudication (fin de siècle) 84 n.16, 348 n.5 (Harvard Univ. Press 1997). For a sophisticated recent statement of the indeterminacy position emphasizing that legal materials are always mediated by the strategic work of interpretation and therefore have no determinate existence "in themselves," see Duncan Kennedy, *A Left Phenomenological Alternative to the Hart/Kelsen Theory of Legal Interpretation,* in Legal Reasoning: Collected Essays 153 (Davies Group 2008).

[2] *See Die Justiz im Dritten Reich,* May 30, 2006, http://www.123recht.net/printarticle. asp?a=16764 (citing a 1936 Berlin civil court case justifying eviction on grounds that being Jewish "undermined the strength of the tenant-house community").

[3] Elizabeth Mensch, *Cain's Law,* 36 Pepp. L. Rev. 541 (2009).

[4] *See* Sanford Levinson, Bush v. Gore *and The French Revolution: A Tentative List of Some Early Lessons,* 65 Law & Contemp. Probs. 7 (2002).

[5] Bush v. Palm Beach County Canvassing Bd. (*Bush v. Gore I*), 531 U.S. 70, 71 (2000).

[6] Bush v. Gore (*Bush v. Gore II*), 531 U.S. 98, 98 (2000).

[7] *See, e.g., id.* at 135-44 (Ginsberg, J., dissenting).

[8] 67 Brook. L. Rev. 1141 (2002).

[9] *Id.*

[10] *See generally* Joseph William Singer, *The Player and the Cards: Nihilism and Legal Theory,* 94 Yale L.J. 1 (1984).

[11] *See* Richard A. Posner, The Problems of Jurisprudence 83 (2007); Paul D. Carrington, *Of Law and the River,* 34 J. Legal Educ. 222 (1984); Louis B. Schwartz, *With Gun and Camera Through Darkest CLS-Land,* 36 Stan. L. Rev.413, 433-34 (1984).

[12] *See* Jacques Derrida, Dissemination 75-84 (Barbara Johnson trans., University of Chicago Press 1983).

[13] *See, e.g.,* Clare Dalton, *The Politics of Law,* 6 Harv. Women's L.J. 229, 234-48 (1983) (book review).

[14] *See* The Beatles, *A Day in the Life,* on Sgt. Pepper's Lonely Hearts Club Band (Parlophone 1967).

[15] William Blake, *Auguries of Innocence,* in The Complete Poetry & Prose of William Blake 492 (David V. Erdman ed., Anchor Books 1988) (1965).

[16] This is among the main themes of my book, Peter Gabel, The Bank Teller and Other Essays on the Politics of Meaning (Acada Books 2000); see especially *What Moves in a Movement?* on page 184.

[17] Bob Dylan, *The Times They Are A-Changin'* on The Times They Are A-Changin' (Columbia Records 1964).

[18] Bernard Weinraub, *30 Years Later, Cake and Credit Cards in Saigon,* N.Y. Times, May 1, 2005, *available at* http://www.nytimes.com/2005/05/01/international/asia/01saigon. html.

[19] *See* Gabel, *supra* note 16, at 87-92 (discussing a full development of these ideas in the chapter, *The Blockage of Social Desire: The Circle of Collective Denial and the Problem of the Rotating Lack of Confidence in the Desire of the Other*).

[20] Martin Luther King, Jr., *Montgomery Bus Boycott,* in Ripples of Hope: Great American Civil Rights Speeches 210, 213 (Josh Gottheimer ed., Basic Civitas Books 2003) (1955).

[21] See Gabel, The Bank Teller and Other Essays on the Politics of Meaning (Acada Books 2000), and especially its chapter 19, *What Moves in a Movement?*

[22] The reference is to the teaching of the Kabbalah that our alienation is expressive of an original shattering of G-d's Divine Light that must be repaired through the work of tikkun olam, the healing and repairing of the world.

[23] Karl E. Klare, *Judicial Deradicalization of the Wagner Act and the Origins of Modern Legal Consciousness, 1933-1941,* 62 Minn. L. Rev. 265, 301-03, 322-25 (1978).

[24] Alan David Freeman, *Legitimizing Racism Through Anti-Discrimination Law: A Critical Review of Supreme Court Doctrine,* 62 Minn. L. Rev. 1049, 1052-57 (1978).

[25] Duncan Kennedy, *The Structure of Blackstone's Commentaries,* 28 Buff. L. Rev. 205 (1979).

[26] Peter Gabel & Paul Harris, *Building Power and Breaking Images: Critical Legal Theory and the Practice of Law,* 11 N.Y.U. Rev. L. & Soc. Change 369 (1983).

[27] Mary Joe Frug, *Re-reading Contracts: A Feminist Analysis of a Contracts Casebook,* 34 Am. U. L. Rev. 1065 (1985).

[28] Anthony E. Cook, *Beyond Critical Legal Studies: The Reconstructive Theology of Dr. Martin Luther King, Jr.,* 103 Harv. L. Rev. 985, 989-93 (1990).

[29] William E. Forbath, Law and the Shaping of the American Labor Movement (1991).

[30] Rhonda V. Magee Andrews, *Racial Suffering as Human Suffering: An Existentially-Grounded Humanity Consciousness as a Guide to a Fourteenth Amendment Reborn*, 13 Temp. Pol. & Civ. Rts. L. Rev. 891 (2004).

[31] *See generally* The Network of Spiritual Progressives, http://www.spiritualprogressives.org.

[32] *See generally* Klare, *supra* note 22; Freeman, *supra* note 23.

[33] *See* David Lerman, *Restoring Justice,* Tikkun, Sept./Oct. 1999, at 13.

[34] *See, e.g.,* Robert A. Baruch Bush & Joseph P. Folger, *The Promise of Mediation: The Transformative Approach to Conflict* 14 (rev. ed. 2005) (emphasizing the transformative power of "recognition"); Gary Friedman, Challenging Conflict: Mediation Through Understanding (2009) (discussing "understanding-based" mediation movements).

[35] *See, e.g.,* Douglas Ammar & Tosha Downey, *Transformative Criminal Defense Practice: Truth, Love, and Individual Rights—The Innovative Approach of the Georgia Justice Project*, 31 Fordham Urb. L.J. 49 (2003).

[36] Emmanuel Levinas, Totality and Infinity: An Essay on Exteriority (Alphonso Lingis trans., Duquesne Univ. Press 1969).

ESSAY FOUR

A NEW VISION OF JUSTICE

From Individual Rights to the Beloved Community

LIKE A ROSE THAT HAS SPROUTED IN A WEED GARDEN and induced the weeds to back away in awe, the Restorative Justice movement has entered American legal culture and is posing an important challenge to core assumptions about human beings and about the very nature of human reality that our legal culture has taken for granted for more than two hundred years. The United States itself was founded on a principle of human freedom that presupposed an inherent antagonism between self and other, a belief that the essential meaning of liberty was that we need to be protected *against* other people. This fear of the other was in part a rational response to the religious, social and economic persecution that had in part characterized previous historical forms of social life, but it also introduced its own distortion into our liberal social fabric: It gave rise to a conception of social being that conceived of human beings as socially separated "individuals" who might form voluntary relationships with others through love, or through contracts, or through voluntary religious and civic organizations, or through democratically elected governments with strictly limited powers, but who at bottom needed always to hold in reserve the memory that the other posed a threat to one's liberty and who therefore required a binding legal culture that placed "the rights of the individual" above all other social goods. Implicit in this worldview has been the conviction that we are not inherently connected beings whose fulfillment comes through our mutual recognition of one another, through the inherent bond of our social nature that is completed through the embrace of love and solidarity, but rather that we are cast into the world as disconnected monads who only come into relation after the fact of our individual incarnations, with the borders between us being in need of constant policing to make sure that the seduction of trust never leads us to let down our guard. While we might "voluntarily" engage in any foolish dependency on the other that we choose, the law is always there to guarantee "as a matter of law" that nothing actually *binds* us except our mutual and solemn commitment to our everlasting ontological separation.

As you read this from within your own private space as you float through the solitude of your day, consider how the institutions of American law condition and envelop you in the spiritual prison of your separation. You are a citizen in a democracy, but the most fundamental right that defines that democracy is the "secret ballot" rather than a process expressive of any communal bond that unites us. You are legally bound to all others through a "constitution" that protects you against, and therefore affirms the constant threat of, infringement on your right to freedom of speech, of religion, of association, and your right to be protected against others searching your house or making you quarter soldiers or taking away your guns...but that binding constitution affirms nothing about our connection to one another and therefore offers no commitment to making sure that our social connection will be realized through our legal process. The substantive law of property guarantees that we can own separate land parcels and exclude others from those parcels, but affirms no binding obligation to share the land, or the food that it produces, or the shelters that we construct upon it. The law of contracts guarantees our freedom to enter binding agreements with others, but in a social context that assumes we are competitors in a marketplace whose goal is to get the benefit of our bargains, rather than "cooperators" whose intention is to realize ourselves through mutual fulfillment and shared objectives. Tort law assures we are protected against others who might pull a chair out from under us as we sit down to the dinner table, or intentionally or negligently harm us on highways or in the operating room or through the consumer goods we buy in their stores, but it does not affirm that we have any duty to care for each other, to rescue each other if we are in distress, or to otherwise act in accordance with a bond emanating from our common humanity. Under the law of corporations, shareholders are assumed to be anonymous investors seeking as discrete individuals to maximize their short-term profits and to be bound to each other solely by that goal, rather than to be socially responsible beings united by a corporate aspiration that will further the well-being of the community or the planet. And finally there is the criminal law, which understands social violence of all kinds as freely-chosen individual acts against the State calling for punishment of the individual actor rather than as social acts expressive of distortions within an inherently social fabric and that call for repair of the social fabric itself.

The conviction that we can only be *bound* by our separation and not by our connection is reflected not only in the substance of law, but also in our forms of legal reasoning and our embodied legal processes themselves. We have learned to equate "due process" with the adversary system, which defines conflicts as contests between opponents who cannot trust each other to tell the truth and who therefore have every right to tear each other down through cross-examination even if one believes the other side is telling the truth. Each side in the gladiatorial combat is encouraged to aggrandize the correctness of his or her own position, to never admit weakness or doubt or frailty for fear of undermining one's case, and to demean and minimize the other side...because that is the only way to absolutely guarantee that no one in the proceeding—neither judge, jury, nor one's adversary—will be taken in by misplaced trust. Evidence is limited to empirical proof of hard facts, past human experiences emptied of feeling and presented as mere observed behaviors, subject to relentless testing for misperception or hearsay, because "allowing in" the meaning and feeling of past events would be inherently subjective and could not be trusted to be presented or heard without bias and distortion. And hovering over the entire proceeding are the rules, with justice being defined as accurate application of the rules to the facts according to an analytical form of legal reasoning—the clever product of the much venerated "legal mind"—that excludes compassion or empathy or care or the aspiration to a world based on love and understanding, and instead valorizes logic and "common sense," the common sense of a world based on individual self-interest and perception of the other as a stranger whose interests clash with rather than complete our own.

As unflattering a portrait as I have painted here of our inherited legal culture, we cannot but recognize the genius that animates it and that unifies all its elements. *If* one wished to construct a binding image of the social world that would maximally protect the individual against all of the possible evils of subjection to the other that have occurred throughout history—slavery, serfdom, the burning of millions of women at the stake for heresy and witchcraft, cruel and unusual punishments like drawing and quartering or the stockades, every form of demonization through superstition and magic—the generations that preceded ours did a remarkable job of inventing a system of justice that was alert to the risk of the threat posed by the other at every turn. And we should admire and embrace the equally remarkable accomplishments that this commitment to individual liberty has been in significant part responsible for—the partial overcoming of the inherited social hierarchies of the aristocracy, and more recently of racism, sexism, and, increasingly, homophobia by gradually eliminating as a matter of law the legitimacy that these stereotypes and negative judgments could formerly claim. While the liberal revolutions of the late 18th century could not directly address and overcome the causes of these forms of social injustice because its own world-view recognizes only the rights of socially separated individuals rather than the need for a legal culture and process to heal the social distortions of an inherently socially connected, interhuman universe, it is nonetheless true that the historical affirmation of the dignity of the individual that was born in the Enlightenment and became binding on us one to the other at the end of the eighteenth century has made an immense contribution to our autonomy from the church, the State, inherited caste systems, and all other ways that exploitation and domination by the other had previously been legally justified.

Yet as we now look out at and live within the envelope of the world we have thus created, we must come to realize by a kind of evolution or enlightenment—by "waking up"—that the liberal framework, the framework of separation, is not only inadequate but harmful. It is harmful because it mischaracterizes a hopeful, potentially loving, potentially mutually confirming and anchoring collective destiny as a destiny of solitudes. And because the liberal world-view is not merely a matter of opinion, but is made binding through law on all citizens, it forms a kind of constant unconscious backdrop that others are receding away from us, that we must pursue our own self-interest, protect ourselves, and endure the pathos of our lives and deaths as solitary beings. Still more, because we in reality are not solitary beings but beings animated by the longing for mutual recognition, affirmation, and love, the liberal world-view inevitably generates a kind of chronic social paranoia that results from the contradiction between the interhuman truth of our social nature and the social message that the other cannot be trusted. As a way of "mediating" this contradiction, of trying to satisfy the need for connection with others in a social world in which others are presented as a threat to our individual safety and integrity, many of us are drawn to grandiose, imaginary collective identities of perfect unity (the Nation, God, the Family, the Gang) accompanied by demonization of other groupings who become the repository of our fear of non-recognition and humiliation, our fear that our own longing for love, acceptance, and recognition will be rejected rather than reciprocated. In this way, the liberal paradigm actually tends to create and recreate the very forms of unfreedom and inequality that in its conscious aspect it seeks to delegitimize and eradicate. Thus as Dr. Seuss suggests in *The Butter Battle Book*, in the world as it is we may use legal means to eliminate racism, sexism, and other traditional forms of demonization only to turn to dividing the world between those who butter their bread on one side and those who butter it on the other.

So as much as we support the great accomplishments of the liberal revolutions and as much as we should continue to fight for the remaining liberal gains not yet won (like the right to gay marriage) within that past and passing paradigm, we need also to support the transcendence of that paradigm toward a new vision of law and legal culture that seeks to foster empathy, compassion, reconciliation with the other, and the fundamental rediscovery that other is not essentially a threat, but the source of our completion as social beings. Along with the remarkable Truth and Reconciliation in South Africa, which demonstrated that a legal process can be used in the service of healing even terrible acts of social violence and which made possible the overcoming of Apartheid without the extensive bloodshed and counter-violence common to prior revolutions, the most significant harbinger of the new paradigm has been the Restorative Justice movement.. The critical difference between restorative justice and the liberal model of justice that we have inherited from prior generations is that restorative justice begins by embracing an ideal of justice not as a blind woman deciding without prejudice which of two equal individuals has the better right to be vindicated under the law but rather with a world view in which we are already in relationship, and in which our greatest aspiration is to realize the possibility of mutual understanding and acceptance through new spiritually alive legal processes that are designed to try to heal the distortions that have masked that possibility of healing and redemption from us.

In contrast to the liberal model with its focus on the rights of the individual person, restorative justice emphasizes the importance of taking responsibility for the well-being of others, performing restitution to those harmed by wrongful conduct, and aspiring to apology and forgiveness as means of reintegrating broken relationships and sometimes knitting together and repairing whole communities. Try to imagine a world in which restorative justice processes are being conducted on a daily basis in the City Halls and other major civic buildings in the center of the cities or towns that you live in. Imagine how much this change in the legal culture of your city or town would alter the way you perceive your neighbors and the spiritual and moral character of communities and neighborhoods that surround you. For it is in the public manifestations of restorative justice that its true social impact will be felt, its capacity to establish through public visibility and legitimacy that we are coming to recognize and publicly acknowledge what we have known and longed for all our lives—that we are in this together, that we are not infinitely and eternally separated by what divides us, and that while acknowledging and respecting the contributions to us of our forefathers, or if you like our "founding fathers," we can risk leaving them behind.

PART TWO

POLITICS:
HISTORY, ELECTIONS, MOVEMENTS

M ANY PEOPLE ASSOCIATE THE WORD "POLITICS" exclusively with elections and the processes leading up to elections, which in today's world involve a central focus on candidates competing for governmental offices, on advertising and marketing these candidates and the cultural manipulations attendant to capturing the votes of a dispersed citizenry, and to a much lesser degree on political parties and their organizations and on party platforms which take largely unknown positions on a limited range of contemporary issues. Through the lens of this very limited focus, it is understandable that many associate the word politics with a feeling of cynicism and even despair—this narrow vision of politics does not involve the vast majority of people in any direct self-activity or engagement with others except for the momentary act of voting on rare occasions, and even that act is carried out in secret, cut off from vital interaction with others about whether the world we live in is a good world and whether we ourselves can transform it for the better. We silently suffer pain, impotence, and even humiliation when the hopes that we invest in this slender collective process of voting, which many think of as their only opportunity to participate with others in the creation of our collective life on earth, are disappointed, casting us back into the privatism of our social separation, re-sealing us in our private routines, and consigning us to four more years of watching public reality on television or our personal computers.

But in reality politics has a much greater meaning than this impoverished vision and is filled with much greater potential than what we can achieve by the occasional act of voting. Politics is in truth the totality of our collective effort to shape the world, and the impoverished conception of politics-as-elections actually reflects a world-view in which we have forgotten and made unconscious our collective strength. In my lifetime, I've had the good fortune to be part of a political movement—the social upsurge of connection that was the 1960s—that ricocheted across the globe in the multiple forms of the civil rights movement, the women's movement, the environmental movement, the gay liberation movement, the student movement, the antiwar movement, the vast anti-colonialism movement, an enormous wave in which, for a time, our collective power to shape and alter the world by our collective, everyday activity became apparent to us—and not just the most active of us, but everyone. Indeed, those who sought then to resist the pull of the sixties toward a universal egalitarian human community based on mutual recognition, love, and spontaneous generosity have in many cases devoted their whole lives to resisting precisely this impulse. As I showed in my book *The Bank Teller*, the entire last thirty years of the Reagan Revolution is best understood from a spiritual standpoint as a revolt against the communal impulse of the sixties, or perhaps to put this outpouring of longing and life-force in a larger context, of the cumulative manifestation of this impulse as it stretched from the thirties through the sixties and continues to express itself today through the evolution of this idealistic hope into the next generations. The Reagan Revolution and the rise of the New Right (no longer so new) has been based primarily on the fear of the other that I explored in both the introduction to this book and in many of the essays in Part One, a fear which expresses itself as a stern, sometimes frenzied resistance to any utopian or hopeful affirmation that mutual recognition, love, spontaneous generosity, and creating a world based on caring for one another as a natural impulse of who we really are as social beings—that such a world could actually be a safe and realistic aspiration for us to strive for. To be sure, the sixties itself helped bring about its own demise because—as I also showed in my essay "How the Left Was Lost" (*The Bank Teller*, Chapter 6)—the very same fear the Right marshals in opposition to "government programs" or gun control or taxation (all of which at bottom are expressions of love and care, of a moral, communal impulse) was also manifested within the movements of the Left as political correctness, lack of compassion, hyper-judgmental criticism, and even a threatening and frightening rage and violence of its own. Still the inherent goodness of the life-force in these liberatory and caring social movements keeps pressing on our own resistance to that very impulse—the force of longing and hope, and also truth, keeps a constant positive pressure on the fear that attempts to contain it.

Seen though this broad and totalizing lens, politics is this entire spiritual struggle, and each of us here in our time on earth either advances the upward spiritual effort, through individual kindness and positive and hopeful social participation, or seeks to contain it, through personal rigidity and various forms of domination and control. Within this flow of the life-force of social movement and the effort to contain that life-force, elections also play a part, sometimes quite an important part, because elections are moments when we all act together to state our collective position on where the balance of hope and fear is at a particular moment in time: elections are like the "declare" in hi-low poker. Over the last thirty-two years since the election of Ronald Reagan, elections have mainly measured the temperature of the water, with hope getting an upward blip, sometimes quite a big blip, with the elections of Bill Clinton and Barack Obama. But when social movements are able to break through the normalizing limits of the social container vessel, when they are able to truly "gather steam" through an upsurge and ricochet of mutual recognition of our true common humanity, the water can boil over and the movement itself recovers its presence and self-awareness as the true heart of politics. At those moments of collective self-activity that is evident to itself and permeated by its own self-knowledge, the true collective nature of politics as the totality of our collective effort to shape our world beyond elections and politicians becomes apparent to all of us.

In Part Two, I try to locate the political flow at three historical points—the year 2000 at the time of the extraordinary moment of the case of *Bush v. Gore*, when the Supreme Court unconsciously evaluated the balance of hope and fear in American society as a whole and decided that it could decide the presidential election in favor of the forces of fear, and then in short essays on the roles played by John Kerry and Barack Obama in 2004 and 2008 in either inflecting or failing to inflect our social confidence in the direction of hope. Since these essays were written at the time of each of these historical moments, they reflect my own attempt as a writer to help move the ball forward at those moments, and the optimism that to some extent may burst through them reflects my sense of what was possible then, not necessarily what seems realistic in retrospect (but the fact that my hope then may seem unrealistic now does not mean that I was wrong then). This part of the book concludes with a description of the importance of social movements and the parallel world we must create alongside the normal one in order to sustain these movements.

ESSAY FIVE

WHAT IT REALLY MEANS TO SAY "LAW IS POLITICS"

The Political Meaning of Bush v. Gore

IN THE EARLY AFTERNOON OF DECEMBER 8, 2000—five weeks into the national debate about who had won the presidential election and four days before the United States Supreme Court settled the matter[1]—San Francisco's 24 Divisadero bus was making its way along its cross-town route. On the surface, everything seemed normal on that bus—the passengers isolated in their passive roles, staring blankly straight ahead or looking aimlessly out of their windows, each avoiding eye contact with the other, proceeding along on the conveyor belt of social alienation that has imprisoned so many of us so much of the time for the last twenty years.

Then suddenly a big guy in a brown leather jacket got on the bus at Haight Street and shouted, "The Florida Supreme Court decided for Gore 4-3!"[2] Instantly, people leaped out of their seats, threw their arms around each other and began dancing for joy, talking to each other and speculating with new hope that perhaps the forces trying to stop the Florida vote-count could be defeated. Eventually, everyone calmed down and took their seats, but they sat closer to each other than they had before and continued to talk, to connect, about the election.

Now that we are sealed in the Bush presidency, it is difficult to remember that in the six weeks between the first Tuesday in November and December 12, 2000, Something Happened.[3] The chaos of Election Night, the wrong calls of the networks, Gore's calling Bush to concede and then calling him back to retract the concession as last-minute Florida vote totals were phoned in to him in his car, Bush's all too human "Do what you gotta do" reply oddly undermining the soft-toned halo with which the media had just presidentialized his televised likeness as it sought to elevate him from mere personhood to George Walker Bush, Forty-Third President of the United States, and then the bafflement of the experts about what was to happen next and the inability of the television anchors to anchor anything—all of this accidentally but decisively disrupted the coherence of what was supposed to be an institutionalized political ritual of which we the people were supposed to be passive, numbly enthralled spectators, just as we had been of the debates and the political ads and the scripted role-behavior of the candidates leading up to the election. And with the dissolution of the object comes the dissolution of the subject—the inability of the election to unfold as "watched democracy," as a numerical activity of "counting to a result" that is the only unity that the common product of isolated and detached voters can have, suddenly and spontaneously released us *en masse* from our reciprocal disconnection as detached spectators and hurled us into a kind of disorganized and exciting engagement with each other. Rather than being an external and alien process in which each of us watches who "the others" elect, with each of us being both observer and "one of the others" in our capacity as voters, the election suddenly became real because we became real. We suddenly became The People.

Today, so many months and so much history later, it is difficult to remember that at that moment, right below the surface, a majority of Americans really cared about the outcome of the election and could have been mobilized to insist that their democratic wish be respected. But that didn't happen. Instead, in part because of what Al Gore and his lawyers did, in part because of the success of twenty years of a conservative assault on our collective hopes and our willingness to believe in the possibility of a new and more connected social order, we succumbed to an outcome which was neither legitimate nor desired.

Understanding how we came to accept a result that most of us felt was wrong and unjust is an important task if we are to avoid repeating such a mistake the next time such a moment of potential mobilization and change arises. Although today as I write these words the conservative world-view seems to have once again coalesced decisively around us, we have an obligation not to let the embers of our collective hope be extinguished, in part by recalling the circumstances that led up to the Supreme Court's final resolution of the election, and through that process of recollection to grasp the meaning of our own (temporary) defeat. We need to try to grasp exactly how we allowed ourselves to be disempowered, how we allowed the spirit expressed on that bus to (temporarily) disappear from public life, and in so doing to restore our collective memory of what was really possible. So let us try to recall and to understand the lost opportunity that was *Bush v. Gore.*[4]

* * *

Most Americans know that there was something wrong with what the Court did in *Bush v. Gore,*[5] the Supreme Court decision awarding the 2000 presidential election to George Bush. They know that we are supposed to be living in a democracy and that it just can't have been legally justified for the Court to have jumped in and peremptorily declared the winner before every reasonable effort had been made to count every vote in every instance where the intent of the voter could reasonably be determined. This widespread sense that the Court majority somehow abused its authority was intensified by the manner in which the Court intervened in the process—overturning the Florida Supreme Court's first seemingly reasonable and brief extension of the certification deadline on the basis of some rarified legal objection that nobody could understand[6] (involving a statutory presumption of validity—a "safe harbor"—afforded state legislative selection of electors), and then a week later blocking a statewide manual recount of machine-rejected ballots on the basis of a completely different legal objection not even mentioned the first time they tried to stop the count from proceeding (violation of the Equal Protection Clause).[7] You didn't need to be a legal scholar to know that Justices Rehnquist, Thomas, Scalia, O'Connor, and Kennedy wanted to stop that vote count and were intent on finding a legal justification for doing so no matter what. It is in fact almost impossible to reconcile the two Court interventions with each other or to find any legal authority for the election-terminating aspect of the final decision.[8]

Yet the meaning of what was "political" about *Bush v. Gore* is not that the Supreme Court failed to follow something called "the rule of law" that is not political. On the contrary, by going so far beyond the legitimate limits of constitutional interpretation, the Court made transparent what is usually mystified—the political nature of all legal reasoning. The political choices made by the Court were possible because Gore and his legal team chose to frame the issues in ways that reinforced a conservative political climate which had been building for the past thirty years. The important task for us is to see how this enveloping conservatism shaped Gore's legal strategy and guaranteed its ineffectiveness—and why Gore and others around him couldn't understand how self-defeating that strategy was.

Voting Rights, Not States' Rights

The core of the legal position chosen by Gore and his lawyers was their decision to base their argument for a manual recount in Florida on "states' rights" rather than on "voting rights."[9] From election night on, it was clear that Gore had won the popular vote by about 500,000 votes, a margin far greater than Kennedy's victory over Nixon in 1960 and greater than Nixon's victory over Humphrey in 1968. He had gained this popular democratic majority through the efforts of African-Americans, women, and working people who had come out to vote in large numbers between 5:00 p.m. and 8:00 p.m. all across the country. These constituencies had all won the right to vote through long and difficult struggles over the past 200 years. They did so in the name of the expansion of the ideal of popular democracy as the very foundation of what it means to be an American. Whatever criticisms and even cynicism these constituencies feel toward the American political system, if they share an idealistic belief about anything in their identification with being an American, it is that they've got the right to vote, that they fought for it, and that it's sacred.

Although the text of the Constitution itself does not guarantee the right to vote, the Fourteenth Amendment,[10] the Fifteenth Amendment,[11] the Nineteenth Amendment,[12] and the Twenty-Fourth Amendment,[13] as well as a long line of venerated Supreme Court cases interpreting them,[14] all affirm that the right to vote is the nation's most sacred political value. Even though the electoral college has retained its place as the means for selecting the president—a power granted to it in the eighteenth century when none of Gore's core constituencies had yet won the right to vote and when states had no obligation to (and sometimes did not) hold popular elections for president—the movement of the last 200 years has unquestionably been toward the expansion of popular democracy carried out by universal suffrage as the basis of political legitimacy.

Against this backdrop, it seems clear that Gore's legal argument for supporting the Florida Supreme Court's decision to allow a manual recount, both in the first and second of his U.S. Supreme Court appeals,[15] should have been that the constitutional right to vote, and to have one's vote counted, is more important than more-or-less arbitrary state deadlines for counting that vote. The central argument of Gore's lawyers Laurence Tribe and David Boies should have been to uphold the Florida Supreme Court on the grounds that their interpretation of conflicting Florida state laws—allowing the manual recounts called for in one statute over another statute imposing a deadline on submitting certified vote totals that would have made the manual recounts impossible—reflected not only a normal and inevitable responsibility of a state Supreme Court to resolve conflicts in state legislation, but also that the Florida Supreme Court acted in a manner consistent with the highest value of the Constitution of the United States—namely, that in a national presidential election especially, the right to vote and have one's vote counted should take precedence over certification deadlines that had little practical or moral significance.[16]

This approach would have aligned Gore's political and moral claims with his legal claim and would have mobilized the constituencies that made up his popular majority. Gore would have been speaking before the Court in support of the universal voting rights of all of us in a democracy, including those of us in the other forty-nine states, rather than making an amoral argument in support of the right of the State of Florida to not be bound by any such compelling universal ethical claim. If he had done this, he would have spoken, for example, for me, one of millions of Nader supporters who voted for Gore at the last minute to keep Bush out of the White House. He would have acknowledged my stake, as a California Gore voter, in whether the manual recount in Florida took place. This was the time to act—at a moment when the right to vote had a genuinely utopian, Walt Whitmanesque, democratic resonance—when the whole country was on the edge of its seat over a matter suddenly filled with vital political and moral American importance.

Had Gore argued for voting rights instead of states' rights, he would have put the Supreme Court in the position of saying to Gore voters across the country, "No, you don't have the right to vote" because of some technical rule (whether that rule was Florida Secretary of State Katherine Harris's deadlines or obscure federal statutory provisions). If Gore had argued for voting rights, the Court's reliance on technicalities would have been accorded little legitimacy in the face of everyone's commonsense assumption that in electing a president, the right to vote should trump such trivialities.

But it didn't happen. Instead, something quite silly happened—namely, that with the entire country focused on what would be said before the Supreme Court, Gore's lawyers said something that nobody could understand. At the very moment when the simplest of arguments would have mobilized and united Gore's national base, his lawyers took a position before the Court that excluded all non-Florida voters, and was in any case incomprehensible to anyone except the lawyer/law-professor talking heads trying in vain to explain eighteenth- and nineteenth-century technicalities to a baffled population who thought this was about the right to vote.

Why? The answer to this question is the answer to the election itself, to why the Court thought it could get involved, why it did, and why it correctly sensed it could get away with even contradictory and irrational decisions to put the wrong man in office.

The answer is that over the course of the last twenty years, beginning with the collapse of the social movements of the 1960s and the election of Ronald Reagan, the Right has successfully and gradually capitalized on the doubt pervading the forces of social transformation in such a way as to make people lose faith in the existence of a hopeful and idealistic universal public sphere in which there is a "We"—an activist and more-or-less united public community—struggling for a better world against the fearful forces of the status quo.

The Reagan Revolution

The heart of the Reagan Revolution was a sort of snapping or reversal of the public energy that had given rise to the Labor movement of the 1930s, the New

Deal, the multiple and overlapping movements of the 1960s (including the civil rights movement, the student/anti-war movement, the women's movement, the gay-and-lesbian movement, and multiple other transformative efforts). Although all of these movements, of course, continue to have positive effects on the larger society, in their universal "movement" dimension they had begun by the late 1970s to be pervaded by what I would call ontological doubt—by a rotating loss of faith or confidence in their capacity to fundamentally transform the world. The dynamics that brought about this worldwide loss of confidence are complex, and I have explored them elsewhere.[17] But conservatives in America, who had begun to really organize against the ideas—all of the ideas—of the Left following the defeat of Barry Goldwater in 1964, were able to seize on this collective doubt and turn it decisively to their advantage. To use a simple but compelling Freudian metaphor, they were able to turn the wrath of the cultural superego against the communal longings of the id.

In the public political sphere, their revolution found its leader in the benign authoritarianism of Ronald Reagan, who, in 1980, was able to unify two idealistic images to forge a new national and international hegemonic base. One was the utopian image of the nuclear family, immortalized in the historical sense of the word in Reagan's "Morning in America" ad that showed a mother holding her newborn baby and promising a restoration of the ideal love that conservatives associate with the family as the only safe location of social trust. The other was a declaration of ideological war against the Evil Empire, which in a formal sense referred to the Soviet Union but symbolically referred to the totality of the movements of the Left as the source of chaos, division, and profound psychic danger.

In the legislative sphere, the revolution took the form of a new and intense opposition to the entitlement programs, whose expansion had begun with the triumph of the New Deal in the 1930s and had continued with the vast expansion of civil rights and social welfare programs born of the movements of the 1960s. Government as a carrier of collective hope and care was replaced by the "army of faceless bureaucrats" from whose coercive power "we" longed to be free again by "getting the government off our backs."

But it is in the legal sphere that we find the seeds of *Bush v. Gore*. While Reagan's election and persona represented the hot moment in which the energy that was the sixties was reversed, the long-term legitimacy of Reagan's revolution required a much more drawn-out process of converting the initial hot political moment into a passively accepted legal order. This, in turn, required the gradual dismantling of the political assumptions that had for fifty years supported the progressive ideals of the activist New Deal state and replacing them with new conservative assumptions about the nature of "our constitutional democracy" and the meaning of "the rule of law" as seen through the lens of the new conservative worldview.

Beginning in the late 1970s with the replacement of the Warren Court by the Burger Court, this shift in legal paradigm was gradually implemented over a period of more than twenty years through three principal doctrinal strategies.

The first of these was the resurgence of "the jurisprudence of original intention" as central to the process of constitutional interpretation. When I attended law school in the years 1969 through 1972, lip service was always given to ascertaining the intent of the framers when interpreting the meaning of the Constitution, but the dominant consensus was that the intent-of-the-framers' view had long since given way to the idea that the Constitution was an "evolving document" that ought to reflect the progressive values inherent in the development of the nation's developing conception of political morality. That the Commerce Clause and the Equal Protection and Due Process Clauses should be interpreted to require, or at least permit, collective governmental intervention in the service of a new, universally accepted conception of social justice was more or less taken for granted as the basis for requiring (or at least upholding), legislatively-enacted progressive governmental action. But following Reagan's election in 1980 and continuing with greater conviction after his re-election in 1984, conservatives— such as then-Attorney General Ed Meese and neoconservative legal intellectuals throughout the legal academy and within the now established post-Goldwater think tanks like the Heritage Foundation, Stanford's Hoover Institute, and the American Enterprise Institute—decisively challenged this liberal orthodoxy, insisting instead that it was the Original Intent of the Founding Fathers, and not the views of random contemporary judges "applying their own moral opinions" that should guide the interpretive process.

The effect of this largely successful shift to Original Intent theory was to invoke the great Image of Paternal Authority to deny the existence of a universally shared, progressive public sphere that provided a political basis for left-liberal constitutional interpretation. Never mind that the drafters of the Constitution were mainly a group of twenty and thirty-year olds whose consciousness was shaped in and by the eighteenth century; they were the "Founding Fathers" whose sanctity and eternal prescience could be resuscitated with such force that Reagan could openly ridicule anyone who spoke the "L-word" ("liberal," for those too young to remember) in support of the constitutionality of liberal entitlement programs or in support of, say, the public right of workers to picket on now properly re-privatized property of the owners of malls and shopping centers.

The second major shift in legal theory and doctrine occurred in the realm of so-called private law with the rise of the Law and Economics movement, providing a new rationale for limits on judicial and legislative decision-making. Against the progressive claims emerging from the social-political movements of the 1930s and the 1960s that human beings are bound together by communal moral and ethical values that must be central to the development of our legal culture, the Law and Economics movement, emerging from the ascendant conservative intelligentsia, has sought to empty legal doctrine of socially-binding moral content and aspirations by reinstating the primacy of the freedom of the isolated individual, who must be free to do whatever he or she wants unless he or she is paid for any legal constraints placed on that freedom by the community (now reduced to a mere collection of other isolated individuals).

Although the humanization of the image of the isolated individual as "he or she" has had ideological power, its true economic meaning has been to rationalize the unfettered expansion of global corporate power by serving as a cultural weapon in support of deregulation. And while in its technical aspects the Law and Economics movement has had only a limited direct effect on the discourse of judicial opinions (with notable exceptions such as Judge Richard Posner of the Seventh Circuit), it has become the dominant ideology in American law schools; it has provided the ideological foundation for near-universal pre-eminence of cost-benefit analysis in corporate and legislative decision-making; and it has deeply influenced the increasing dissolution of the use of moral discourse in common-law decision-making in such private law areas as contracts, torts, property, and corporations. In the context of the gradual legalization of the Reagan Revolution, it has contributed importantly to the disintegration of popular belief in the existence of a legally recognizable and public moral community by supporting the image that, apart from the sanctity of the private family and equally private religious affiliations, "we" are a nation of individuals legally bound each to the other only by money, by economic self-interest.

The third major doctrinal shift that has served to gradually legalize the Reagan Revolution—and the one of most direct relevance to understanding the Supreme Court's interpretive strategy in *Bush v. Gore* and to the political capacity of the Court majority to decide the 2000 election in the way that it did without a popular revolt—has been the rise of the "new federalism." Emerging originally in the jurisprudence of the Burger Court in the late 1970s[18] and with greater confidence following Reagan's first election, the new federalism has been, at one level, simply a return to giving much greater deference to states' rights in constitutional interpretation. But in a deeper sense, the doctrine signaled a shift in the official imagery within American legal culture of how "we" are politically constituted as "a people" within the meaning of the Constitution as an authoritative document, a shift to a kind of eighteenth-century idea of the nation as a confederation of sovereign and separate groupings (or states) who have reluctantly granted limited powers to the whole (the federal government).

Originally, of course, the states did emerge out of the colonies as organic groups divided from one another by geography, culture, religious conviction, economy, and even to some extent language. As such, they were understandably reluctant to subordinate their group integrity and sovereignty to a remote national government—that is, a remote national president, legislature, and court system— which, although in principle "representative" in nature, might well come to use its overarching power as the spokesperson for the United States to threaten the moral authority and self-sovereignty of each state. The role of the electoral college in selecting a national president, with its allocation of two senatorial votes to each state regardless of population and its guarantee of a disproportionate voice in presidential selection to smaller states, reflects precisely this concern (among other concerns, including a fear of popular democracy) about the potential "tyrannical" imposition of an alien national power upon the sovereign states who were the source of that power.

But the rise of the new federalism over the last twenty years has no authentic relationship to this historical reality of eighteenth-century life. Virtually no one today feels distinctively identified in the eighteenth-century sense with the state as one's organic group. On the contrary, the political history of the last 200 years has been the growing association of democracy with belonging to one nation, to one culturally diverse but nevertheless economically, politically, and culturally integrated group called the United States of America. Wars, technology, geographical mobility, immigration, the socio-economic development of an integrated capitalist market following increasingly uniform legal rules and norms, the development of national social movements transcending regions as well as states, and many other historical influences have forged a new and concrete historical reality that has decisively subordinated the state as the locus of group-identity and belonging to our national identity, to "being an American."

Thus we invest far more meaning in national elections than state elections and attribute far greater emotional and political importance to American citizenship than to often transient state citizenship. It would be absurd to claim that the core meaning of participation in our constitutional democracy today derives from our connection with the state-based identifications underlying the confederation-based conception of strictly limited federal power of 1789.

The rise of a new federalism which rests on this claim of state-based identifications as the basis of constitutional democracy must therefore be understood as a largely successful attempt to resuscitate the image of 1789 federalism and to imbue the image with the same mystique of cultural authority that has been projected onto the Founding Fathers and the search for their Original Intent. These images draw their fantasy-power from the rituals of our social conditioning since childhood, from the pledge of allegiance to the venerated annual telling of our origin story in childhood civics and American history classes to the sanctified repetition of the names of the Founding Fathers (the side flap of my cereal box once boasted, "TOTAL™ brings you Founding Father James Madison") to the awe and sense of idolatry attached to the Constitution itself as a hallowed document in a glass case whose ideas are somehow "above" those of us mere mortals who have followed those who penned them.

If we recall that what we are analyzing here is the legalization of a conservative revolution designed to reverse actual flesh-and-blood social movements aiming to give fundamentally new meanings to who "we" are, new meanings to the "constitution" of our political and moral bond, the use of authoritative cultural images that we have all been conditioned to feel we are supposed to invest with "belief" is the legal analogue to Reagan's "Morning in America" ad. In the context of the Reagan Revolution and its aftermath, these authoritative and reassuring images seized upon the anxiety that had come to pervade a real world beset by political/moral/cultural/generational/ economic/racial/sexual conflict, especially as collective doubt came to corrode the idealism of the movement that had both generated this conflict through its transformative impulse and vision and given the movement in all its diversity its transcendent and hopeful unity. And because of their power in our shared cultural memory, these images can be and were appealed to in order to persuade "Americans" to come home.

In sum, the common aim of the resuscitation of Original Intent theory, the Law and Economics movement, and the new federalism has been to employ authoritative group fantasies about the origins of America (as the political group to which we each belong) in the service of erasing the constitutional legitimacy of a universal public sphere that leaders like Martin Luther King Jr. and the social movements of the 1930s and 1960s claimed was the very essence of true "constitutional" politics. It was in that universal public sphere in which moral questions about our common group life were and are contested. By mobilizing millions of people in the name of "We the People," social change movements became the living embodiments of democratic ideals as they physically and spiritually occupied this public sphere and challenged the political legitimacy of existing arrangements and constitutional doctrines by seeking to give them a new and progressive moral content.

The Collapse of Socialism

In its temporarily successful effort to reverse that energy, the central element of the conservative legal strategy has been to close down that public sphere. The core image of America projected by the new conservative legal order is that of an individualistic society characterized by a private sphere driven by material self-interest and a de-politicized public sphere comprised of morally unconnected and passive citizens, obedient and deferential to the strict authority of their Fathers. The significance of the "legal" character of this image is that calling it "Law" makes it "binding" on our collective national consciousness. Its gradual internalization has legitimized the privatization of American culture post-1980 and has contributed decisively to confirming the collective doubt to which I referred earlier, the sense that if you get involved and go out into public claiming your democratic authority to change the world, no one will be there for you because there is no longer any "there" there, no longer any "constitutional space" where Martin Luther King Jr. and millions of other Americans once stood.

To this legal history one other central fact must be added, an event that cleared the field for the more or less unchecked development of this conservative worldview. That event was the collapse of the Soviet Union and of socialism as an idea. For 150 years, the idea of socialism had been the dominant worldwide metaphor for the possibility of a fundamentally different world based on community rather than self-interest and the separation of self and other. Every progressive social movement of this century in some way defined itself in relation to the idea of socialism because however much labor or women or the 1960s counter-culture or environmentalists or any progressive person agreed or disagreed with the specific tenets of Marx, socialism's basic affirmation that the world could and should be based on social connection and egalitarian community provided a crucial link between any particular progressive reform within the "whole world" of capitalism and the possibility of a radically different universal social vision and "whole world" toward which particular limited reforms were aiming.

In addition, the fact that the Soviet Union and the socialist bloc actually existed and had been able to mount a protracted long-term challenge to the capitalist ethos all over the world provided the idea of socialism with at least some embodied reality, however distorted, anti-democratic and even brutal that reality was in its existing incarnation. As events have shown since the collapse of the Soviet Union in 1989, even the modern Democratic Party had depended since its origins in the New Deal on being able to define itself as the alternative, liberal-democratic path to the humane social vision to which socialism aspired. Without the moral ideal of community that socialism as a metaphor had come to stand for, and without being able to make the claim that it offers the gradual democratic path toward that ideal that is the correct alternative to totalitarianism, the Democratic Party has no anchoring moral worldview to distinguish itself from the Republican's whole-hearted embrace of capitalist self-interest—except to appear to be the party of half-hearted capitalist self-interest, which is hardly the basis of a compelling moral and political vision that one can expect people to follow.

The fact is that after Stalinism, Mao's cultural revolution, the Khmer Rouge, and the direct experience that millions of people had of the unsafe group dynamics that undermined the (otherwise wonderful, hopeful!) 1960s, nobody could believe any longer that seizing economic and political power from private individuals on behalf of the collective through some apocalyptic revolution could possibly lead to something better than the lives we lead now, however isolated, alienated, and meaningless they often are. So by the early 1980s, the socialist idea had lost its capacity to serve as the unifying communitarian counter-vision that had made the Left a powerful and morally compelling force, and when the principal embodiments of "really existing socialism" vanished from the earth in 1989, the ideology of individualism appeared to have "won." The effect of this was both to give increased legitimacy to capitalism's economic, cultural, and political expansion on an increasingly global level and to greatly weaken the ability of the longing for community (a longing which exists in everyone) to even be seen or heard by the other, much less to be mobilized into a movement based on that longing that could enter public space and make moral claims on behalf of a universal, transformative alternative to an apparently vindicated conservative worldview.

The void left by the collapse of socialism as the dominant political metaphor for community intensified the ability of the American conservative legal intelligentsia to carry out its doctrinal disintegration of the constitutionally-binding public morality that the progressive movements of the 1930s and 1960s had fought for. And, in fact, there is no better testament to the effectiveness of their effort to gradually convert the Reagan Revolution into a new legal order supported by a new and widely accepted conservative "common sense" than the inability of Bill Clinton to make his long presidency stand for anything. Elected and enormously popular precisely because of his ability to recognize and validate our universal longing for community, a capacity that arose in significant part from the effect on him of the civil rights and other movements of his youth, Clinton was forced to rely throughout his presidency on personal charisma and polling data that demonstrated his private popularity among otherwise disconnected individual voters to enable him to survive politically in a public sphere totally dominated by his conservative opponents.

Bill Clinton embodied hope, idealism, and communal aspirations—as the cliché goes, "he made you feel cared about"—but he could not speak for this ideal and aspiration in the name of a coherent moral and political vision. That is why the Right was able to crush his initially popular call for universal health care; he had no coherent social vision with which to fight for it in a public sphere now dominated by an individualist political worldview, a worldview which the Clintons ended up deferring to by basing their legislative strategy on seeking support from the American Medical Association, the private insurance companies, and amoral, implausible claims of cost-efficiency.

Although things might have been different if Clinton had been able to imagine a new, emerging, spiritual-ecological-communal successor to the now-defeated Left and liberal materialist alternatives, he was, in the end, able to do no more than to cut his party's losses by rejecting the no longer resonant communal metaphors of the past ("the era of big government is over"), and, in an act of true political schizophrenia, use his personal capacity to evoke warmth and idealistic hope in the service of expanding the globalization of capital and international trade agreements like NAFTA that consolidated the power of international, private corporate power. In response to the uninterrupted progress of the conservative ascendancy in the social/political/legal sphere, he consistently took positions that actually accepted the conservative viewpoint and merely sought to restrain its influence, defending affirmative action, for example, with such morally toothless slogans as "mend it, don't end it," and signing the Republican welfare-reform bill in return for temporary concessions by the Right to ease their assault on remaining elementary legal protections for labor and the environment.

Increasingly during the course of his eight years in office, he was reduced to defining his legacy as "having presided over the greatest economic expansion in history," an expansion that demonstrated America's ability under his leadership to "compete and win in the world market." Taken as a whole, this record actually strengthened public acceptance of the continuing normalization of the Reagan Revolution, precisely because it showed that even a popular, liberal Democrat seemed to accept the inevitability of its basic tenets, and even measured his own success by conservative "free market" criteria.

The Weight of History

By the time of the presidential election of the year 2000, the Democratic Party no longer felt capable of even appealing to its own constituencies on the basis of a progressive social vision. Having been forced to kneel at the Republican altar for so long, even former participants in the movements of the 1960s like both Bill and Hillary Clinton abandoned the transformative convictions that had shaped them (and that were still visible in both of them as late as 1992), not because they no longer cared, but because they had nothing to say, no way to translate their social idealism into a new political idea.

Non-movement liberals like Al Gore, who were influenced by the 1960s but remained fundamentally loyal to mainstream political values, more fully retreated to the half-hearted conservative worldview. So 2000 found Gore running a presidential campaign that was merely a pragmatic "less bad than Bush" laundry-list of disconnected, centrist proposals, like prescription drug benefits for the elderly, increasing standardized testing to prepare the workforce for the new global marketplace (but requiring fewer such tests than Bush), and touting "cost-effectiveness" and a greater ability to correctly "add up the numbers" as the basis for distinguishing his Social Security and Medicare proposals from those of Bush.

Behind the moral impotence of the Gore campaign was a now thoroughly conditioned acceptance that whatever transformative political ideals once defined his own life personally and the convictions of his party were now irrelevant, that these ideals could no longer move "We the People" to leave their private houses and private self-interested concerns and enter the public sphere to provide a popular base for a contagious and winning campaign. As a result of this long process of devolution that I have described and the popular internalization of a politically passive, conservative political worldview, Gore understandably may have believed that while he might win the election by a lesser-of-two-evils campaign if he could get his already organized constituencies to get out and vote, he could not rely on anyone to be there for him if he invoked F.D.R., Martin Luther King Jr., and the great egalitarian and communal traditions of his party's past.

Thus when the amazing occurred on Election Day and woke up the American electorate from the now thoroughly legitimated and seemingly inevitable prisons of their private and isolated routines, Gore was ill-prepared to mobilize a suddenly intensely politicized national community. Like someone who hasn't gone to the gym for twenty years and is then suddenly expected to be in shape, Gore and his advisors were themselves so demobilized by twenty years of political and moral inactivity that they were incapable of grasping the opportunity that the accident of the election results and the ensuing six-week national debate about the meaning of democracy had handed to them. All over the country, friends were talking intensely on the phone and strangers were talking intensely on street corners about Florida and the right to vote and Katherine Harris's attempts to stop the vote count. High-school and college students actually focused for the first time in their lives on the electoral college and its ability to trump the popular vote, intensely discussing and struggling to understand the seemingly anti-democratic justifications for it.

Within a matter of days, a constitutional democracy that had come to see itself as but a collection of privatized, passive, and disconnected individuals suddenly emerged into a fledgling, but genuine, political community hurled into common public engagement by the threat that even the right to vote—the very foundation of American democracy won across centuries through an intense moral struggle and at the cost of many lives—might be denied in determining the outcome of a national presidential election whose democratic legitimacy is supposedly entirely based on it. Within a few days after November 7, and for a period lasting almost six weeks, Americans were galvanized by the one moral imperative and shared moral bond that even the most conservative government could not take away from them—the shared moral certainty that their government's legitimacy rests on the will of the people. While the act of voting every two or four years can often seem to the isolated individual like the most minuscule act of public self-assertion, the idea that the right to vote could be taken away was a challenge to the deeply held moral ideal of democratic self-determination. During the period from November 7 until December 12, when the Supreme Court ended the matter, the challenge to that moral ideal was sufficient to allow the false "we" of a deferential and isolated people to begin to emerge into a real "we"—an active, collective presence ready to demand its sovereign birthright.

If we now see this dramatic period following November 7 in the historical context that I have described, we can understand the collective "political unconscious" underlying this drama as a struggle between conflicting impulses existing within each individual and within the national community as a whole. One was the fearful impulse that had sought for twenty years to block the desire for social connection and for a just, egalitarian, and erotic community from again becoming a public force. The other was the utopian democratic impulse—the Walt Whitman impulse in "I Hear America Singing"—that was accidentally and spontaneously released by the closeness of the election and the controversy about how it would he resolved.

The fearful impulse was reflected in the frantic efforts by Katherine Harris, James Baker, and others to stop the Florida vote count immediately by strictly interpreting a trivial deadline for certification of Florida's vote totals and by constantly repeating to a suddenly aroused and empowered national community the mantra that "there had already been recount after recount" in order to prevent the manual counting of uncounted votes. This fearful impulse also was reflected in the panicky assertion by some across the country, but especially those in the Bush campaign, that "we've got to know who our president is." I call these "fearful impulses" because they were plainly irrational—there was no pressing need to know the outcome; at stake was the outcome of a national presidential election, the most important single incarnation of our democratic process. In the past Congress has counted state electoral votes received as late as January 6 (the day of the counting).[19] The Constitution and federal law even provide for a custodial presidency by the Speaker of the House if there is a delay beyond January 20 in accurately determining a presidential election's outcome.[20] Florida's certification deadline was obviously intended merely to provide a uniform date to guide and coordinate in normal circumstances a schedule for statewide counts, rather than having some substantive importance that might justify certifying an inaccurate result.

But it was the palpable pressing need to "know who our president is" that best reveals the nature of the fear, a fear analogous to, say, "not knowing who our Founding Fathers are." It was the fear that the closure and de-politicization of public space that had been so central to the political imagery underlying the new Right's "constitutional interpretation" would be threatened the longer that the absence of a presidential authority figure left this public space open. This was especially true because the spontaneous release of the right-to-vote popular democratic impulse was creating a sense of passion and excitement with unknown consequences. Without quickly "installing a president" and normalizing the nation's political structure, no one could be sure what would bubble up in the vacuum. Thirteen-year-olds might start asking their parents just what the point of this electoral college is, and didn't Gore win the popular vote, and how can Katherine Harris claim to be objective Secretary-of-State and vote-counter when she was co-chair of the Florida Bush for President Committee, and what about those African Americans I heard were intimidated by the police? The longer the political space remained opened, the greater the risk to the legitimacy of a conservative worldview that for twenty years had relied on the passive acceptance of what I earlier called Paternal Authority.

However, it was Gore, and not the Republicans, who posed the greatest obstacle to the success of the popular democratic impulse. Having long since left behind the days when he liked to smoke pot, grew his hair long, and went off with his girlfriend in a canoe on a 1960s-inspired journey in search of the meaning of life, Gore had run a campaign that remained well within the reigning conservative paradigm, offering no progressive moral vision of any kind. That in itself made it difficult to rally behind him in the post-election contest as the idealistic champion of the people and of popular democracy. But what made the situation worse was that he had been so demobilized and co-opted by the devolution of idealism of the previous twenty years that he himself did not realize in the post-election period (and I'm sure could not believe or trust) that the people who generated his substantial popular vote majority were trying to cast off the enforced isolation and political inertia of those twenty years and mobilize to fight for him in the name of democracy, of the right to vote. Most Americans thought the Republican efforts to stop the recount were wrong, thought that Katherine Harris's repeated attempts to stop the count on the basis of a purported objective and neutral exercise of her discretion were patently absurd, and they believed that, with a fair and full count, Gore had probably won.

But instead of emerging publicly and speaking passionately on behalf of democracy to and for his own voters, a known majority of the country, Gore assumed the same posture as Bush, behaving like a remote presidential candidate, making occasional formal public statements at which he took no questions, insisting that the vote-count question was a legal matter to be handled by his lawyers and the courts, and otherwise holing-up in the vice president's mansion and allowing rare photo-ops of family touch-football games. Instead, he could have come out and thanked the working people and women and minorities who had poured out to vote for him after working all day in crucial cities like Philadelphia and Los Angeles and Miami, exercising their democratic right to vote for which men like Martin Luther King Jr. fought and for which so many had lost their lives. Had he linked their exercise of that right to his fight to have every vote counted in Florida, Gore would have seized the high moral ground, mobilized his constituencies, and thoroughly discredited the efforts of James Baker and the Bush team to use every method—including the threat of physical violence in the case of the Republican-organized riot outside the Miami-Dade county registrar's office—to impede democracy's most sacred principle. He also would have made the Florida state legislature's threatened decision to simply appoint a slate of Bush electors, irrespective of the outcome of the popular vote, appear shamefully undemocratic, rather than being legitimate as technically legal under Article II, Section 1 of the Constitution.[21] By opting instead to try to "act presidential" and turn the whole matter over to highly paid lawyers, Gore sacrificed his chance to seize the moral initiative on a matter that he himself deeply believed in, and allowed the media to characterize him as no different from Bush, with both sides represented by an army of lawyers and both motivated simply by their own self-interest. He also left his popular majority rudderless while significantly marginalizing the political importance of his substantial popular-vote victory. By failing to see that his true political community were the actual people themselves who had just voted for him, rather than the version of the people represented in the image of constitutional democracy prevailing in the now decisively dominant conservative worldview, he actually created the conditions that legitimized his own defeat.

Who Are "The People"?

This last point deserves emphasis and provides us with the most important lesson to be drawn from the 2000 election regarding the relationship between politics and law. When the United States Supreme Court made its first intervention in deciding the outcome of the election by taking certiorari in *Bush v. Palm Beach County*,[22] it informed the lawyers for both sides that it wanted them to address the question of whether the Florida Supreme Court's first decision to extend the time for the initial recount through the Thanksgiving weekend violated either Article II, Section 1 of the U.S. Constitution or the series of federal statues in 3 U.S.C. governing the federal certification of state electors to the electoral college.[23] That request indicated that the Court majority intended to evaluate the legality of the Florida Court's decision by measuring it against a version of how "the people" were "constituted" according to political values prevailing between 100 and 200 years ago.

In doing so, the Court was calculating, consciously or unconsciously, that the American people of today, who had just voted in a democratic election for the nation's highest office and had elected one candidate by a 500,000-vote majority, would nonetheless accept the legitimacy of a decision by the Court to decide the election in favor of the other candidate based on its interpretation of a version of the democratic will of the American people drawn from the legal materials of a much earlier and very different time. For example, the dates in the federal statutory provisions regarding certification of state electors, one of which the Court eventually used to award the presidency to Bush without allowing completion of the Florida vote-count, were based on how long it would take to deliver lists of electors from the several states by horseback to Washington D.C.[24] Similarly, the political values shaping the version of "the people" reflected in Article II Section 1—the basis for the Court's unanimous reversal of the Florida Supreme Court in the first case[25] and the concurring opinion by Justices Scalia, Thomas, and Rehnquist in the second case[26]—would have denied the right to vote to a very large percentage of Gore's voters.

The only reason that the Court majority felt they could take the risk of intervening on this basis was that they guessed, at the time of their first intervention, that they could use their fetishized legal authority as the supreme interpreters of the Intent of the Founding Fathers to superimpose their eighteenth-century version of the people on the people themselves, even though the real human beings comprising the people as a living, democratic, national community had just spoken. From the standpoint of any present-day understanding of the political meaning of popular democracy, it was ridiculous to assert that the Florida Supreme Court was prohibited from allowing a few extra days to obtain an accurate vote-count that would determine the outcome of a national election. Of course it was permissible, and even essential out of respect for the will of voters nationwide, to extend a more-or-less arbitrary counting deadline to figure out, in accordance with the statutorily expressed policy of the Florida legislature, which candidate the people of Florida had really voted for. Yet by channeling the political meaning of constitutional democracy into a legal framework drawn from an era when some states did not even allow popular votes in presidential elections, and by then commandingly posing supposedly knotty and abstract legal questions that "smuggled in" these antiquated political assumptions while appearing to be both rational and complex from a legal point of view, the Court majority guessed it could use its twenty years of accumulated conservative cultural capital to "awe" the people into another, imaginary, political world. And because the Supreme Court's authority is precisely to declare what political world is also the legal world, its opinion would be accepted as binding on the community as a whole.

Had Gore and his liberal lawyers been able to see and trust the reality of his own national democratic base—by speaking before the Court for them on the basis of the universal moral ideals of the present day embodied in the right of everyone to vote, and emphasizing in the name of leaders like Martin Luther King Jr. precisely the overturning of states' rights restrictions on that highest of democratic values that had marked the Court's jurisprudence since at least the Civil War—he might have mobilized his really-existing People in a way that would have overwhelmed the images of the "people" relied on by Bush and the Court majority. Against him, he would have had the twenty years of loss of faith that would have made it difficult for his popular majority to believe there was still a hopeful public space to emerge into, and he would have had the media, which until such a popular democratic reality succeeded in emerging, would have projected the inevitability of the Court's image of Authority to speak for the People (consider the media's fascination with the awesome architecture of the Supreme Court's chamber, the fact that we the people were going to be "allowed" for the first time to hear their allegedly devastating questioning of the lawyers, and the frantic scramble to get seats for the oral arguments in which the Great Ones would appear in their full regalia, emerging from their secret and sanctified private chambers where their supposedly majestic conversations about the nature of our constitutional democracy occur, conversations which the average people actually constituting that democracy could certainly not understand). Overcoming the cultural power of these images would have been difficult; so long as the post-election contest remained mainly a media event in which people could only connect as a people by watching television, these images provided powerful psychological support for the twenty-years-in-the-making closure of and even erasure of the popular-democratic space that the Gore majority would have to reclaim. But had he and Lawrence Tribe and David Boies stood up boldly in the name of Martin Luther King Jr. on behalf of the right to vote, I think the Gore forces would have succeeded in allowing the present reality of the people to defeat the long-dead version of the people on which the Bush forces and the Court's conservative majority depended.

But instead of standing up for voting rights, Gore and his lawyers meekly pleaded for states' rights,[27] the traditional Republican metaphor that has been used for centuries to deny working people, women, and African Americans the right to vote. Of course, in their public statements outside the legal sphere, Gore and his spokespeople did invoke the right to vote as the basis for their call for a full and fair Florida vote count.[28] But by severing this political claim from their legal claim, they decisively undermined their ability to claim that the right to vote was not just their view of the right principle to be followed, but was also the universally binding moral ideal that the Court was obligated to recognize as binding upon a national community founded upon the will of the people.

So enveloped were Gore and his lawyers in their own belief in the power of the conservative worldview, so weakened was their conviction that there really was a People out here to support their own political viewpoint, that they allowed themselves to think that they had to argue from a position of weakness: to cling to the hope that by being "good boys" and dutifully framing their legal argument in the antiquated version of the People that the Court majority had for so long successfully been constructing, they might have a chance of pleading with either Kennedy or O'Connor to vote with them and thus eke out a five-to-four victory on states' rights grounds. ("See, Justices, we recognize your authority and your worldview, and we humbly ask that you decide for us on those grounds.") By doing so, they effectively limited the meaning of the legal debate to morally trivial, technical legal questions affecting only Floridians, and dissolved the emerging unity of their own national democratic base by depriving us of our ability to claim constitutional legitimacy—in the name of our own national democratic majority—to demand that the Florida vote count proceed.[29]

Once Gore and his lawyers deferred in this way to the conservative worldview and its version of who the People were, we were lost. Ironically, by the time the Court finally ended the election in its second decision on December 12, 2000,[30] the Court itself had to bow to the national popular pressure that had built up on its own on behalf of the pre-eminence of the right to vote over the six-week period of nationwide political debate and shifted its rationale from their initial strict reading of Article II, Section 1, to a rationale based on equal protection theory.[31] Undoubtedly, the Court majority knew that the two Court decisions read together were incoherent and unsupportable. But they also knew that there was no longer any possibility of a unified public majority empowered by a publicly articulated sense of constitutional entitlement that could do anything about it.

Even if Gore could not have changed the outcome of the Court decisions and of the election itself by uniting his political and legal claim under the transcendent banner of voting rights, he would, by doing so, have posed a powerful challenge with significant popular support to the long conservative assault on the very existence of a socially-connected, national community demanding legal recognition in the name of the highest of democratic values. Instead of the political demobilization and isolation that so envelops us and separates us from each other today, we and they would know that we exist, that we claim to be legitimately "constituted," and that by quite a large margin we had and have the votes.

CHAPTER NOTES

[1] Bush v. Gore, 531 U.S. 98 (2000) (holding that standardless manual recounts violated the Equal Protection Clause of the Fourteenth Amendment).

[2] Gore v. Harris, 772 So. 2d 1243 (Fla. 2000) (holding that Gore satisfied his burden of proof with respect to the Miami-Dade County Canvassing Board's failure to tabulate, and therefore ordered a hand recount of the 9,000 ballots in Miami-Dade County).

[3] See Joseph Heller, Something Happened (1974).

[4] 531 U.S. 98 (2000).

[5] Id.

[6] Bush v. Palm Beach County Canvassing Bd., 531 U.S. 70 (2000).

[7] See generally Bush v. Gore, 531 U.S. 98 (2000).

[8] See Bush v. Gore, 531 U.S. at 123 (Stevens, Ginsburg, & Breyer, JJ., dissenting).

[9] See Brief for Respondent at 43-50, Bush v. Gore, 531 U.S. 98 (2000) (No. 00- 949) [hereafter Brief for Respondent].

[10] U.S. Const. amend. XIV.

[11] U.S. Const. amend. XV.

[12] U.S. Const. amend. XIX.

[13] U.S. Const. amend. XXIV.

[14] See, e.g., Oregon v. Mitchell, 400 U.S. 112 (1970) (and cases cited therein).

[15] See Bush v. Gore, 531 U.S. at 98; see also Bush v. Palm Beach County Canvassing Bd., 531 U.S. at 70.

[16] In failing to assert the centrality of the constitutional right to vote in supporting the Florida Supreme Court's interpretation of state law, rejecting even the existence of a federal question and defending only the appropriateness of that Court's reliance on Florida's state-based right to vote in resolving the statutory conflict, the Gore argument presented an image of the U.S. Supreme Court as powerless to authoritatively declare the substantive moral correctness of the Gore position. Thus had the Florida Supreme Court decided for Bush, Gore's stance would have left the U.S. Supreme Court powerless to reverse on the basis of the moral pre-eminence of the constitutional right to vote. The mobilized political moment required Gore to affirm the Court's constitutional authority to decide for him in the name of democracy and to make a "call" upon the moral and legal responsibility of the Justices to do so. See infra text accompanying notes 27-29.

[17] See Peter Gabel, "How the Left Was Lost: A Eulogy for the Sixties," in Peter Gabel, The Bank Teller and Other Essays on the Politics of Meaning 78-82 (2000).

[18] I foretold the political meaning of the rise of the new federalism and its relationship to "legalizing" the Reagan Revolution in "The Mass Psychology of the New Federalism:

How the Burger Court's Political Imagery Legitimizes the Privatization of Everyday Life," 52 Geo. Wash. L. Rev. 263, 270 (1984), in which I wrote: "The Court's aim is precisely to make the New Right constitutional . . . by reconstituting the existing hierarchy-system within an imaginary framework that conforms to a new 'intent of the framers.' For in the long run it is only by transforming the recent wave of right-wing activism into a passively accepted legal order that the new conservatism can become a genuinely dominant ideology in the way that democratic liberalism has been for most of our recent history." (emphasis in original)

[19] Jack M. Balkin, "Bush v. Gore and the Boundary Between Law and Politics," 110 Yale L.J. 1407, 1421 n.55 (2001).

[20] 3 U.S.C. § 19(a) (2000).

[21] U.S. Const. art. II § I states: Each state shall appoint, in such manner as the Legislature thereof may direct, a Number of Electors, equal to the whole Number of senators and representatives to which the State may be entitled in the Congress: but no Senator or Representative, or person holding an Office of trust or profit under the United States, shall be appointed an elector.

[22] Bush v. Palm Beach County Canvassing Bd., 531 U.S. 1004 (2000).

[23] Bush v. Palm Beach County Canvassing Bd., 531 U.S. 70 (2000).

[24] Larry Lipman, "Challenge Planned to Electoral College Congress to Make Count Official Today," Atlanta J. & Const., Jan. 6, 2001, at A3.

[25] Bush v. Palm Beach County Canvassing Bd., 531 U.S. at 76.

[26] Bush v. Gore, 531 U.S. at 112.

[27] Brief for Respondent, at 50.

[28] "Vice President Al Gore, News Conference on Florida Election Lawsuit" (Nov. 28, 2000), transcript available at http://www.pbs.org/newshour/bb/election/julydec00/-fl_11-28.html.

[29] See Bush v. Gore, 531 U.S at 98.

[30] Id.

[31] Id. at 103-10.

ESSAY SIX

WILL THE REAL JOHN KERRY PLEASE STAND UP

FOR JOHN KERRY TO WIN IN NOVEMBER, he needs only to do one very difficult thing: find his true self and manifest it as a moral presence. The current John Kerry does not yet exist as a compelling moral presence. Instead he is afflicted with the disease that has plagued Democrats for two decades—the disease of "positioning himself."

Positioning oneself is a way of not actually standing for something from the inside out, but rather trying to manipulate one's outside to appear to be the person whom you hope "the majority" wants you to be. When John Kerry intones, in his best stentorian voice, "From North to South, from East to West, all across this great country, the message is clear; the people want change," he is trying to "sound like" someone, but he is not actually being someone and not actually speaking—"lights on/nobody home," to quote the Talking Heads. A sound that merely sounds like something conveys only hollowness; John Kerry only echoes himself rather than manifesting a true presence, the presence of a really existing moral being.

Moral presence, authentic moral conviction, is essential in a leader (or if you prefer, a spokesperson) because what we as a society suffer from most acutely is moral entropy—the experience of floating in an ether disconnected from others and from active, meaningful alignment with the social world. If we can't connect to each other in compelling, meaningful, life-giving ways, we must endure what the poet Wallace Stevens called "the malady of the quotidian," the routines of a passive everyday life in which we feel we are just going through the motions of living, merely watching the killing in Iraq, for example, and feeling a true moral agony at being unable to understand this killing as real, to engage with it, and to act to influence it. When we merely watch the world, we suffer terribly from being unable to link up to it, encapsulated and imprisoned in our unmoored and floating minds.

George Bush does have moral presence, and it may lead him to victory even though most people find his presence disturbing and his moral direction flawed. Uptight and anti-erotic, he is most at home when he is in angry pursuit of his idea of righteous vengeance. But he is genuine in the sense of actually being there: "He stands at Armageddon and he battles for the Lord." And for the floating listener in need of a moral anchor, Bush "comes across," even if the hand he extends is not the hand the listener wants to grasp. Never mind that most people do not agree with his simplistic good-and-evil worldview. For those trapped in a moral vacuum, he offers a way out, and an imperfect way out is better than no way out. George Bush does not render himself a ghost by positioning himself.

John Kerry will lose by five to ten points unless his constituencies come out to vote between five and eight pm on election day. But people will not be pulled to the polls unless Kerry does the pulling with a moral presence more compassionate, more complex and clear-headed, and more embracing of the moral hopes of humankind than the presence offered by Bush.

We are all waiting for the John Kerry who risked his life to save others, who led the Vietnam Veterans Against the War, who as a young man courageously testified before Congress about the brutality and immorality of our violence toward the Vietnamese people, and who at one time gave as much as he could of himself to help us create a just and human world. Each time we listen to him we are hoping that this earlier John Kerry will emerge through the hologram, the handsome persona, the mouther of stentorian clichés, and by becoming present himself allow us to emerge into a group and become morally present to each other through the mediating role into which history has thrown him.

If he does this, he can't lose. If he doesn't, he can't win.

ESSAY SEVEN

BECOMING PRESENT

MY ADVICE TO THE 2008 PRESIDENTIAL CANDIDATES IS AS FOLLOWS: Read Eckhart Tolle's *A New Earth*. Seek to quiet your monkey mind as it races from what to say to this group, what to say to that group, how to deal with the media, how to deal with your staff, what to do about the polls, while containing your anger at public mischaracterizations of your views.

Seek to become Present. Present as you talk to your staff and the media about what you believe. Present as you address a human community through the media. Present as you face each of the thousand natural shocks of a presidential campaign.

The single most important source of suffering for the people that you are speaking to and seeking to lead is not their fear of physical harm for themselves and their loved ones, and not their fears about the economy or lack of health care or any other material need: it is their experience of disconnection from a substantial, meaningful, authentic reality.

Surrounded by people who are always keeping their distance by averting their gaze and playing this or that artificial role, bombarded by messages from this same artificial environment telling them they are somehow lacking in this or that quality or attribute, bathed in media images whose predominant emotion is cynicism toward everyone and everything, the people that you are speaking to are longing to be anchored by the presence and authenticity of a compassionate and loving spokesperson for the group who confidently projects his or her energy toward the possibility of our creation together of a compassionate and loving world.

To manifest that presence is your job. Nothing else.

Becoming present will be challenging for you because you must conduct your campaign through a mediating screen of images that will resemble the fun house at an amusement park, except that there's nothing fun or amusing about it. Everything you say will be subject to distortion as it passes through the ether of media scrutiny. Those who cannot embrace your manifestation of authentic presence and the call for authenticity that implicitly accompanies it will seek to cynically undermine your every word and gesture. And since you cannot control the process by which your views and character and aspirations are stolen from you and replayed in alien form to sectors of the population whose votes you may need to win the election, you will be pressed by your staff to be more and more careful, to constantly "position yourself," taking account of the spin that is about to be put on your words, to move to the center independent of your actual convictions, to stand for as little as possible and still win because the more strongly you stand for something the easier it is to make the consequences appear to lead to some kind of "disaster."

The mediating screen of images through which you must pass to reach the real human beings you are addressing is constituted by the very same impulse toward doubt, cynicism, and collective flight that has placed your actual listener in his or her isolation, his or her spiritual prison. But that anxious circulation of doubt and fear about whether it is possible to connect with others in an authentic loving and compassionate way is precisely what your listener longs to be liberated from. And that mediating ether of doubt and cynicism and fear and flight from one another is made of "nothing" besides its own noise. Your own capacity for love and compassion can penetrate it because it is made of something, your very own presence.

This then sets for you your task: Become present as a manifestation of love and compassion for your human listeners who long most of all for the affirmation of this presence in themselves but who can only be brought into contact with it by having it "recognized"; project your presence through the mediating environment while taking account of the environment's distorting effects without altering Who you are; and create a mandate for bringing closer the world that we all know ought to be.

ESSAY EIGHT

OBAMA AND THE FLAG PIN

WHEN BARACK OBAMA STOOD OPPOSITE Hillary Clinton during the Pennsylvania debate without his flag pin on, he was actually being an American hero. Practically inviting the inevitable exposure of his naked lapel by debate moderators George Stephanopolous and Charles Gibson, Obama was willing to stand with the authenticity of his being against a demand that he adhere to a false image of "we," and hope that by doing so we could all break through to another level of connection to our common humanity.

In truth, all of us watching the debate have longed from birth to enter into an authentic relationship of mutual recognition with the other, with all other beings. This desire is at the very heart of our social nature—it is the foundation of every baby's search for eye contact, for sensual nurturance and holding, for the completion of the self that only occurs through the reciprocity of authentic connection.

But tragically for all of us, we are born into a world that is not fully "there" yet. For a complex of reasons, as much as we long for each other, we are in flight from each other, passing each other with blank gazes on the street, hiding behind artificial self-presentations that we ourselves monitor moment to moment to keep each other at a safe distance. In place of the authenticity of mutual presence, we condition each other to take on the artifice of this or that "role;" and in place of the authenticity of a supple and vulnerable human community, we require each other to pledge allegiance to a common mental image of community that blankets a universal solitude.

Thus the flag pin. When Obama stands before us as a candidate for president without his flag pin on—in his birthday suit, so to speak—he is appealing to all of us to trust that we can come out from behind our wall of coercive images and take the risk of being there for one another as who we really are. And when Stephanopolous and Gibson draw a threatening attention to the fact that he is not wearing the pin, they are actually expressing their anxiety that Obama might succeed, that if he were to become our leader, we might all be expected to become present to each other in a true relation of I and Thou as a loving and vulnerable humanity (themselves included). Thus although they are quite possibly liberals "in private" and do not privately believe that presidential candidates should be required to wear certain pins, in their public roles as "objective" journalists, they chose to engage in a false neutrality that sought to police Obama's ethical intentions on behalf of "the American People." Against Obama's courageous manifestation of and call for authenticity, the role-playing journalists chose to try to isolate the man and collude with the fearful image-world that supports, that actually is, the status quo.

Nothing that I'm saying here is meant to denigrate the value of patriotism as an identification with the best aspects of American history and culture, and Obama's willingness to challenge a coercive form of flag idolatry is in some ways a distinctly American accomplishment. I like the way Obama sometimes wears the flag pin and sometimes does not, showing respect for the cultural achievements of the historical community that he seeks to represent while resisting any fixed and robotic deference to a false image of community that traps all of us in a painful spiritual isolation. In some ways, the very best aspect of Obama's campaign has been the quiet confidence with which he has maintained his autonomy from the cascade of challenges to his "loyalty" that have underlain not just the flag pin drama, but also the uproars over Reverend Wright, Bill Ayers, and Bittergate.* That autonomy is not really about separating himself from irrational and unfair allegations; it's about reaching out toward us through an invisible ether and affirming that we are all really Here and that a less crazy, more loving, more real world is possible.

---

* "Reverend Wright," "Bill Ayers," and "Bittergate" refer to three political crises that occurred during Obama's first presidential campaign. Reverend Wright was a controversial pastor whose church Obama attended; William Ayers was a former leader of the radical sixties group The Weathermen, with whom Obama had served on a Chicago based non-profit decades later; and Bittergate was the term given to the controversy that followed Obama's having said at a private party that some rural Pennsylvania voters who had faced long periods of unemployment and depressed economic conditions would naturally "cling to guns or religion or antipathy to people who aren't like them or anti-immigrant sentiment or anti-trade sentiment as a way to explain their frustrations."

ESSAY NINE

Memo to Obama: How to Avoid Becoming Co-opted

This is the first of three essays on Obama, written as a memo shortly after his first election when the country, or at least his supporters, still felt intimate enough with him to call him "Barack." In retrospect, this first essay might be called "the Moment of Hope"; the second might be called "Disappointment"; and the third, after Wordsworth, "Resolution and Independence."

Dear Barack,

The outburst of tears, joy, hope, and worldwide celebration that we have all witnessed and been part of in the days following your election is a beautiful expression of what you and we have accomplished at this historical moment— namely, a breaking through of the years of sedimented fear, doubt, and authoritarian control that have separated us from each other and from our most idealistic aspirations for humankind. The integrity and authenticity of your human presence spontaneously called forth a desire in all of us to reciprocate by emerging from decades of doubt-filled isolation and social separation to create a circuit of energy sufficient to ricochet one another into a sweeping electoral majority in support of the possibility of creating a more loving, humane, socially connected, and spiritually elevated world.

Because you so consistently expressed this elevating possibility through an even-tempered steady confidence, you were able to pierce the veil of media distortions that sought to deflect and falsify your idealistic vision. You did so with enough force to successfully reach all of us out here in our disparate locations, and to touch and mobilize our own longing for a better world. Spurred by a vast circle of affirmation mediated through you, we each became a force vector for each other, leveraging us to volunteer in large numbers to make manifest our own collective presence and lay claim to a new idealistic future.

But watch out! No sooner had we begun to catch our breath following the euphoric moment of seeing "Barack Obama Elected President of the United States" flash across our television screens, than the force of fear, which rotates through our collective consciousness with lightning speed, had begun to take up its fall-back position, seeking to assimilate your victory to the status quo. Its method is to subtly rob that victory of its potentially transformative meaning and replace it with a safe meaning, in order to insure that the socially separated world—the fearful world of detached and withdrawn isolated individuals—does not in fact change.

The ideological technique that the force of fear has begun to adopt to try to assimilate and co-opt (y)our victory is to declare that what happened on November 4 was the demonstration that an African American can now win the presidency of the United States. This casts the meaning of the election as a victory for nondiscrimination, as if what we were all celebrating was merely that anyone can now compete for and win the presidency without regard to race. The corollary of this interpretation will be to test how well you are doing as president by analyzing not how transformative your leadership is but rather how conventional it is—by how well you manage the government, how well you manage foreign affairs, how well you manage the economy, or in other words, by how well you "play the role" of president within a system that is otherwise supposed to go on functioning the same as it ever was. It is in accordance with this very narrow interpretation of the meaning of your victory that so many conservatives (from George Bush, to Condoleezza Rice, to Brent Scowcroft) have hailed November 4 as a historic moment; that CNN asked as its first call-in question to its listeners after the election whether your victory should signal the end of affirmative action; and that so much early coverage of your presidency has addressed such conventional role-based matters as what new styles Michelle will bring to the White House or what kind of puppy you will get for the kids.

While the fact that racial discrimination did not keep you from being elected is of course a very good thing, that fact in itself is not the reason why so many of us cried at the moment of your victory, or why Kenyans spontaneously danced in the streets and declared a national holiday, or why young people all across the country are wanting for the first time to get involved in politics and change the world. The transformative meaning of your election is rather that you are the carrier of the great egalitarian social movements that have preceded you, movements that aspire to a world in which we can recognize each other's whole humanity and love each other across our racial differences, in which a new ethos of social justice and beloved community can replace the selfish world of individualism and fear of the other that has led to the proliferation of wars and the death by starvation or malnutrition of 20,000 children per day, and that in some measure consigns us all to a lifetime of spiritual isolation and passive social meaninglessness.

A confluence of forces came together to make your victory possible—from the surprise collapse of the economy that trapped your opponent John McCain into identifying with the policies that created the collapse while opening up a new space for you as the youthful and spirited agent positioned to change these policies, to the weakening, after three decades, of the reaction against the sixties that had fueled the rise of the New Right's traditional God/family/country-based worldview and rendered unsupportable liberal openness, compassion for the other, and the very existence of a public sphere animated by a moral vision for a more just and connected world. This confluence created the political conditions for you to grab on tight to your own hope and idealism—expressive of the social movements that preceded and helped shape you—and to then "thread the eye of the needle" on election day by successfully carrying forward your own grounded ethical presence right through the web of false statements, doubt-mongering, and potentially compelling false images of who you actually are that were deployed in the effort to use the inertia of the long conservative hegemony to derail and undermine the expansive life force that was your momentum.

My message to you is this: resist the attempts to normalize your presidency by putting you on a pedestal of nondiscrimination, isolating you as "the leader," and then gradually tearing you down after your absorption into isolation has demobilized your base. Instead, follow these four principles to help strengthen your base and deepen the meaning of your presidency:

1. Recognize that your election represents a collective effort to transcend selfishness and individualism. Take every opportunity to give voice to what you have already called "this new defining moment" as a moment of love and care for one another. Reject the Republicans' "ownership society," which you have already made fun of as meaning "you're on your own," and make clear your own conviction that "we're in it together." Express the meaning of your decisions and policy commitments in exactly these idealistic terms. Even more, indicate that this turn toward each other represents an evolutionary moment in American history, away from the exclusive preoccupation with individual rights that characterized the beginning of the republic and toward a new ethos of empathy, compassion, and connection between self and other. The brilliance of your early speeches after your initial victories in the primaries was precisely that they linked the meaning of your campaign to the upsurge of social concern that was manifested in the abolitionist

movement and then as an upward tendency in all the great social movements throughout American history—upward movements which taken as a whole have produced you yourself as an ethical manifestation of their aspirations and convictions. Now that you have won, give voice to this higher meaning by explicitly linking what you do in our name to going beyond individualism toward community.

2. In order to make manifest this idealism and upward movement in the context of specific issues, always give expression to the spiritually deep intention and purpose of each specific policy proposal. For example:

• When advocating for Social Security, make it clear that you are standing up for one of history's greatest manifestations of intergenerational care and concern, rather than letting yourself be pulled into "how will we fund it" debates that fail to evoke its high moral purpose.

• When explaining the selection of new Supreme Court justices, make it clear in what way the person you have appointed is a practitioner of justice concerned with the well-being of all of us as embodiments of a common humanity. Choose an appointee who will interpret the law in accordance with the wisdom, compassion, and social concern expressive of the moral bond that unites us.

• When recommending new legislation to pull the economy out of its current crisis, make it clear how the reforms you propose represent a new governmental ethos that understands "we the people" as a mutually supportive community, rather than as a scattered collection of self-interested, competitive individuals.

• When advocating for educational reforms, indicate how these reforms will advance the spiritual and moral well-being of the next generation as caring and compassionate citizens, rather than simply allowing education to be defined as the mastery of skills needed to compete in the world economy.

• When proposing environmental reforms like limiting carbon emissions or defending the Alaskan wilderness, give voice to the sacredness of the earth and the beauty of the natural world and our stewardship of it for future generations, rather than simply referring to the importance of reversing global warming as a scientific phenomenon.

3. When appearing in public at news conferences or in giving speeches, pay attention to the symbolic elements in your self-representation

by consciously signaling your continuing commitment to idealistic and transcendent meanings. For example, when giving a news conference on the economy, don't only have financial experts like the Secretary of the Treasury or the head of the Federal Reserve present with you on the stage—also have representatives of labor, the environment, and the community as a whole to signal that interventions you will support will be taking account of our collective human and ecological well-being ... and that care for the other remains at the center of your consciousness, no matter how apparently "technical" a proposed intervention (like a "bailout" or a stimulus package) may appear.

4. Maintain the meditative quality that has been perhaps the most distinctive aspect of your public presence throughout your campaign. Captured in the slogan "no drama with Obama," this quality of remaining underneath the hype of the moment has been immensely significant in transmitting the confidence that you are actually here with us on the planet rather than being elevated into an artificial, puffed-up, narcissistic role that customarily captures politicians and removes them from the realm of the real. By retaining this meditative presence, or groundedness, you convey that we really do exist as a "we," and that the publicity enveloping you has not stolen you from the realm of authentic being and the spontaneous social concern that authentic being inherently carries within it. The more successful you are at retaining this authenticity, the less successful will be the attempts to separate and pedestalize you as The President and to isolate you from the authentic community of hope that actually elected you.

I sincerely believe that if you follow these four principles and think through all your actions with them in mind, your efforts will be successful no matter what events and circumstances befall you. I believe this because at the deepest level your task is to build upon the communal confidence, love, and hope that has elected you. What you actually are is the unity of this confidence as it rises up to throw off the fear of the other that has been inherited from prior generations—or more precisely you are the democratically elected leader of this confidence. And you and we together are its unity as it tries to rise up and throw off the fear of the other that has thus far undermined its full manifestation. Half the responsibility for that future embodiment of love is yours and the other half is ours, is mine. I hope we are beginning a new chapter in seeking to move each other toward that good end.

ESSAY TEN

"YES, WE CAN"?

IT'S NOW BEEN TWO WEEKS SINCE THE MIDTERM ELECTIONS of 2010, and I'm noticing that many folks I know are depressed—not consciously about the elections, which have receded somewhat from view, but about various things in their lives. One is exhausted from all the pressures in her life, raising children, caring for parents, working too hard or too aimlessly; another is undecided about what to do next in life, not sure how to chart a meaningful path. Everyone has his or her personal story.

But behind all the personal stories and giving unity to the feeling of despair are the elections—not because of the specific legislative consequences of the Republican victory but because of what it means for the state of whether "we can" or "we can't," or of whether "we" exist at all.

Elections evoke a great deal of passion even though their direct practical consequences for our lives are often minimal, even nonexistent. A huge struggle takes place culminating on election day, but what is the struggle really about? My own practical life—the details of my everyday physical existence—is almost completely unaffected by the outcome. I have the same work, the same family, the same friends, no matter what the outcome. So why all the brouhaha? Something huge appears to be at stake? But what?

The answer is that elections are crystallizations of the emotional field. Like the "declare" in high-low poker, the election is a moment when we tell each other whether we will or will not extend ourselves to each other, whether we believe in our connection and dare hope to realize it in community enough to declare it, or whether we do not and dare not.

There have been times when I've carried my longing to the polling place like a great burden on my back, knowing that although I was going to put it out there when I cast my ballot out into the universe, my gesture would almost certainly not be reciprocated by enough others to make the national declare an announcement of the opening of our hearts. There have also been times, a few, when I had a spring in my step because I had a sense that due to a happy confluence of historical forces, people were ready to take the risk of making themselves vulnerable to their longing for … each other.

Such a moment occurred when we came out into public and elected Barack Obama in 2008, but that moment … call it a "we-moment," a moment when we decided through the act of voting to announce ourselves and so to come into existence as an idealistic, hopeful, potentially loving community…that moment has been slip-slidin' away ever since. Why? Not because we one-by-one ran back into our withdrawn private worlds, but because Barack decided not to reciprocate our vote by remaining out here/there with us, because he was afraid of the vulnerability himself and the risk of some catastrophic negation of his essence if, as he feared, we were not here/there after all.

The election two weeks ago was the end. No more slip-slidin'. We declared the 2008 moment officially over. And quite frankly, there was a major weakness in that 2008 moment—namely, that it was constituted by a media event, by six months of watching Barack Obama on television, by an over-reliance by each of us in our separate space on watching that remarkable smile and listening to that sometimes-transcendent oratory. Our "Yes, we can" was not constituted out of our own social movement, emerging from our own idealistic actions over time through which we stitched ourselves together in real social relations. It was mainly a cheer led by one person through the medium of a television screen. Without his "mediation," we didn't exist.

For the moment, it's "No, we can't." The election makes it official that the "we" that is constituted in public space through a national election is for now a socially separated one; we've announced to each other that we've returned to a state of mutual distance, to one-and-oneness, to the pact of the withdrawn selves. The 38 percent turnout of registered voters in 2010 declares that many of us were too humiliated after extending ourselves in 2008 to get out and vote, to get out and hope. The blank space left by that exhaustion and pain has for now been filled up by the angry impulse, the expectation of betrayal that was waiting in the wings and leaped out onto center stage in the form of the Tea Party and Fox News and Talk Radio. That impulse said "No, you can't," and in our humiliation following our two-year free fall, we went along with it.

It's a relief in a way because we don't have to hang on for dear life to 2008 anymore, and considering that this time we had to declare in the middle of a spiritual hemorrhage, we even showed some signs of toughness and resilience— the victories of Jerry Brown, Barbara Boxer, Harry Reid, Andrew Cuomo, Patty Murray, and the governor of Minnesota and some others. It doesn't matter that those particular politicians may not embody our highest values. It's a sign that there are still some of us, perhaps enough of us, to be part of a new base or "manifestation," who were willing to show up in bad circumstances.

So it's back to the drawing board. This time we need our own movement, our own parallel universe through which to ground our recognition of each other and our longing for an idealistic, high-spirited, loving community. We don't have to write off Barack Obama, but we obviously can't depend on him or wait for him to whirl around toward us (although that could happen). Perhaps he can be part of what we create now—I hope so. But it is We who have to find a way to re-emerge from our reciprocal isolation, from our cast-away withdrawn state, with more bottom under us this time, a bottom provided not by watching the same leader but by a common venture whose meaning we ourselves ground and internalize. Caring for each other's health and well-being, a cooperative economy, no war, "awe and wonder at the grandeur of creation"—in other words, change we can believe in, rather than floundering around in convictionless clinging to what somebody else's televised image might or might not utter today.

When we start to move, to manifest ourselves in a new forward-motion of mutual recognition of who we really are and what we really long for on this earth, our private personal depressions will lift all at once, replaced by the affirmation of each other's presence in public space.

ESSAY ELEVEN

THE SOCIAL MOVEMENT
AS A PARALLEL UNIVERSE

IN "YES, WE CAN"? I ARGUED THAT THE RESPONSE of progressive forces to the Republican victory and the depression it has generated should be to form ourselves into a "parallel universe" to provide ourselves with an independent base or ground on which to stand and recover from the unrequited hope we extended to Barack Obama in 2008. Some readers mistook this to mean that I was suggesting withdrawing from the existing political world into some kind of private space or respite from the existing system, when what I meant to say was that we now have to recover our collective social being from the dependency "we" developed on Barack Obama at the time of the euphoria of the 2008 election. I put "we" in quotes because the unity formed at the time of the election was a thin band of reciprocating recognition mediated through and too heavily dependent on all of us watching Mr. Obama on television during the six-month period from the start of the primaries through the presidential election. The dissolution of that thin band, which achieved some finality in last November's midterm congressional election, has cast us back into isolation and the pain of disappointed hope attendant to that, but it also has created the opportunity to re-form into a more solidly constructed form of mutual recognition, which is what is actually required for us to be effective in changing the world.

As I wrote in my essay "What Moves in a Movement?" (*The Bank Teller*, Chapter 19), a social movement can only emerge and gather steam as a social force if it acquires the density of authentic mutual recognition, if through our participation in it we gain a new sense of our social worth, power, and authority in our very collective being. In a social movement, no one actually physically moves anywhere; the word "movement" actually refers to the acquisition of social gravity that results from the invisible force of a new kind of authentic mutual recognition, a vitalization that occurs collectively through a new inter-experience that provides the ground or support for new idealistic social values. Values without this ground are mere concepts, indeterminate abstractions like freedom, equality, and community that can mean anything and that are given their actual meaning-in-the-world by the life force (or lack of it) present in the social field that gives rise to these values and expresses them in public. What moves in a movement is the life force that animates it and that in turn results from the authenticity of mutual recognition—of spiritual communion and understanding—that provides the movement with its social weight and capacity to influence the social field as a whole.

For a movement to gather this force and to gain the influence to bring about social change, it must find a way to form itself on a ground independent of the society of the whole, and yet within that society. The problem with the Obama victory was that it generated a very widespread but thin unity that could only have brought about the "change we can believe in" if Obama himself—who was excessively responsible for the initial unity as the charismatic mediating embodiment of it—had remained fully expressive of the transcendent idealistic quality that we saw in him long enough for actual groups to form in support of him. This would have required a conflict-filled initial two years in which Obama would have had to fight for an idealistic new vision against the Republicans and Fox News and the cynical "reality police" (as Michael Lerner calls them) long enough for pro-Obama groups to have formed on college campuses, for movement-building demonstrations to have emerged in public space, and for other forms of social activism to have achieved manifestation in new group formations that could then have provided the embodied collective life force to alter the social energy field. Obama's failure to provide that leadership in a circumstance that was totally dependent on him has revealed the inherent weakness or vulnerability of that initial situation, and the recent elections have officially deflated our collective balloon. Unsupported by a wider movement stitched together and vitalized out of real and consistent public activism, the Obama moment has expired without Obama, leaving us facing in mutual solitude the awareness that in these circumstances, "No, we can't."

However, the very failure of the Obama moment can serve to remind us that it is we ourselves who must provide the support within social being itself for our hopes for a loving and idealistic world. To say that a social movement must emerge in a "parallel universe" is to say that a new sense of We must arise as a quasi-independent source of personal and social identity alongside our social self within "the system," within the existing social nexus in which we occupy conventional professional and familial roles. Many of us experienced this side-by-side double reality during our youth in the movements of the 1960s, when the culture felt palpably contested as a struggle between two social and existential realities: "our" reality, which for a time was based on a transcendent sense of social connection and possibility, and the inherited reality, which was more artificial, fear-filled, and even robotic in its social quality. Our movement reality was in this sense parallel to the received one but also engaged with it, in struggle with it, and making demands of it that are still being negotiated to this day in a social space influenced by the pull of both worlds and by the ongoing struggle of hope versus fear that distinguishes these two worlds.

To continue to fight for the transcendent spiritual-political vision, to give it new life and to spark a renewed confidence in it, we must find a way—probably mainly not through the media—to anchor each other in social space through our own parallel and autonomous rotation of recognition and solidarity, through our own liberatory circle of mutual confirmation. It is on the basis of this that we will reacquire the collective strength to emerge from our current withdrawn state and to exert actual "pull" on the empty and artificial mutuality and chatter that out of fear demands that we give up our utopian longings and accept the leveled-down state of the world as it is. When we engage in *tikkun olam*, we stand together in a future space and pull the present toward it, but on the basis of a present, felt intimation of that future that is not itself dependent on the world as it presently is. In just this way, a mountain climber throws his pick upward well beyond where he or she currently stands to gain an anchor point ahead, and then uses the taught line thereby established to measure each step of his or her forward motion.

PART THREE

PUBLIC POLICY

PUBLIC POLICY IS OFTEN ASSOCIATED WITH A DULL AND DETAILED LISTING of arguments that one can make for and against a particular course of action—thus the term "policy wonk" to describe the bespectacled analyst of social problems who makes the reader or listener want to run the other way. This is often a fair criticism because it is so often the case that discussions of public policy are detached and dry affairs that fail to move the reader or listener in one direction or another, that lack moral force. But it is precisely the thesis of this book that social reality itself is moral in nature, that as spiritual beings we are at every moment motivated by spiritual longings and that the very purpose of social activism is to move the world in a direction more likely to bring about a more open-hearted, loving social space and the cooperative, redistributive consequences that must result from that opening up to the other as a Thou. This means that discussions of public policy can't be detached and unanchored to any moral dimension, with facts and arguments piling up on either side of some neutral, passion-free decision to be made on the basis of a purely rational calculation. Instead, we must see with our hearts as well as our minds, grasp the meaning of whatever it is that we are observing and trying to influence in a good way, and then develop spiritually and morally informed policy interventions that make a positive outcome most likely to happen—and even more important, enable these outcomes to become manifestations of the desire for mutual recognition and the overcoming of the denial of that desire. Good public policy and impassioned moral vision can't be separated without depriving the policy, in thought and action, of its rootedness in our spiritual and moral being.

Consider the issue of social security. The public debate about how and whether to fund social security has been continuing for the last fifteen years in a manner largely devoid of moral vision, with the Republicans arguing that it's too expensive and the Democrats arguing that we can afford it and that it won't go bankrupt for several decades so it should be left alone ("kept in a lock box" as Al Gore repeatedly advocated in his 2000 presidential campaign). Within this impoverished moral framework, social security is presented as if it were a lifeless "thing" that we can either afford or not afford, like a car. At most, supporters of social security sometimes make the point that older people are vulnerable and need protection, but even this way of seeing creates an image of "the senior" as an isolated figure gradually wasting away and facing death, a mere "individual" who can't work anymore and for whom the rest of society should have compassion. Imagine how different the public debate would be if social security were spoken for and understood as a great historical step forward in human community, a manifestation of intergenerational solidarity, love, and connection, through which each new younger generation is able together to care for its elders—their parents and grandparents—beautifully affirming that we are in this world together rather than alone. That was the moral purpose of Social Security as articulated by Franklin Roosevelt and his Secretary of Labor Frances Perkins when they first fought for its passage in 1935. And if the progressives of today could recall the spiritually binding power of such a moral discourse and call upon that power to shape their policy proposals, they would quickly build the base of a new social movement.

The essays in Part Three build upon this and other public policy proposals on education, the economy, and the environment that I briefly outlined in Essay Nine, which addressed how Obama needed to speak for his policy proposals if he wanted to be a visionary and transformative president. In Part Three, I extend this spiritual-activist approach to other areas, showing how it is possible to spiritualize our approach even to such "hard" subjects as foreign policy and the natural sciences. The first essay written on the eve of the (second) war in Iraq proposes that we see through the nation-state conception of so-called foreign relations, and instead see the legacy of fear of the other and the social alienation through which that fear is manifested as a kind of inflated reciprocal paranoia that must be "thawed out" and "surrounded" by interventions that allow the underlying aspiration of people for peaceful understanding through authentic mutual recognition to become visible and gain traction, spiritual traction. This does not necessarily mean that the antagonists themselves are the first to reach this higher awareness, but rather that spiritually inflected actions may alter the larger social "climate" within which any nationalist conflict is enveloped so as to allow deeper and more transcendent human longings to emerge and influence the antagonists indirectly.

The essays on science recall my essay "Creationism and the Spirit of Nature" (*The Bank Teller*, Chapter 4), which shows the way that the very "scientific method"—or scientific way of seeing—that Darwin brought to observing living beings limited and distorted his theory of evolution in a way that excluded the spiritual dimension of living organisms and the influence of that spiritual dimension on the process of evolution itself. We are more than just survival-oriented organisms out-adapting each other through natural selection in a dog-eat-dog world, and these final essays of this Part argue for an approach to evolutionary biology that allows that in-dwelling and loving dimension of "the species" to become visible.

Part Three's remaining essay on the fear of gay marriage was written just as the movement toward gay marriage was beginning. The transformation of national attitudes toward gay marriage since then supports the compassionate view of the fearful heterosexual that I try to present in this essay, and in a way offers a mini-example of how the spiritual concepts of "thawing" and "surrounding" that I present in the essay on foreign policy have actually worked within a few short years to begin to heal centuries of antagonism toward gays and lesbians.

ESSAY TWELVE

SPIRITUALIZING FOREIGN POLICY

As the war in Iraq now becomes a daily reality and the deadened-to-human-life consciousness of Bush/Cheney/Rumsfeld and the parade of the CNN generals and the killing headlines of the morning papers envelops all of us in the shadow of our fallen common humanity, we must take a deep breath and try to lift ourselves out of this shadow—not only by engaging in acts of resistance to the war but also by thinking our way out of the paradigm that accounts for war-consciousness and for the deadness to human life that is married to it. This deadness both produces war-consciousness and is produced by it, and it perpetuates itself over and over again from war to war, from generation to generation.

In *Tikkun* magazine, we have been trying to develop for many years now a new conception of spiritual politics that understands the world as a nexus of inherently social human beings linked to one another by more than the individualistic and material needs that have dominated prior political, economic, and social theories. We have claimed that we are each expressions of a loving energy and are animated by the desire for mutual recognition and affirmation of that loving energy—that we each long for recognition of our inherent worthiness and sacredness. We have also sought to analyze the social alienation that obscures this spiritual longing—the need to hide from the other behind masks and roles, to guard ourselves against the humiliation of a nonrecognition and rejection too painful to bear. We now know that it is this alienation of I from Thou, between I and Thou, within I and Thou, that keeps dragging us back into the shadow, and that accounts for the deadness, at the surface of the skin, in the constriction of the heart, and in the flattening of the perceptual field of the withdrawn mind's eye.

We must now apply this understanding to the development of a new conception of "foreign policy"—a term that I dislike because the other is never "foreign." The term implies that we belong to a "we," represented by the nation-state, which is also imaginary to the extent that its function is partly to mask our isolation, to deny our alienation from the person next to us by insisting on our patriotic connection "in the sky." In spite of my dislike of the term, however, I will nevertheless use it here to try to help us imagine a new method of relating to the other in the world that understands itself through the nation-state prism—keeping in mind, however, that the "foreign policy" that emerges from our vision of spiritual politics requires that we never see the other as "foreign." Let's say that I am using "figures of speech" to communicate, but please imagine I am always keeping the quotation marks.

A foreign policy that emerges from this vision of spiritual politics understands that the present situation cannot be reduced to simple formulas that exclude spiritual understanding—the longing for authentic mutual recognition and affirmation of our fundamental humanity—that forms the basis for our vision. It's not just about oil, or about the risk of terror and weapons of mass destruction, or about "lunacy," for that matter. Rather, at the heart of our problem is a complex historical process of distortion in the relation of self to other that *encompasses* oil, and genuine concern about terror, and even an element of lunacy if it is understood to mean the distortion itself gone out of control.

In *Tikkun*, we've often described this distortion as expressive of an historical disease of individualism and materialism, manifested in the competitive global market and in political systems that channel the frustration of the isolated individual into demonization of the other. In the case of the Middle East, we rightly emphasize, for example, that historical dynamics dating back to the Crusades and certainly to the pre-World War I carving up of the Middle East by imperial Western powers, followed by the gradual development and expansion of globalization and capitalist markets, have contributed not only to material poverty in the Middle East but to the humiliation and degradation of entire cultures. This humiliation has contributed—sometimes with direct Western assistance because we perceived it to be in "our" interests—to the emergence of dictatorships and royalist antidemocratic regimes in places like Iraq and Saudi Arabia. This same humiliation of the other's fundamental humanity has inspired the rise of fanatical fundamentalisms that artificially restore a humiliated people's sense of worthiness, meaning, and purpose by glorifying the martyrdom of the suicidal killing of the humiliator, the imperial power who, degraded and fearful inside, becomes the source of the other's humiliation.

The key, as I see it, to the process of hopeful elevation, to lifting ourselves out of this System that we are all entrapped in, is to grapple with and begin to understand the meaning of *tikkun olam*, or the healing and transformation of the world. We must, with a heart that can think, grasp how the process of historical distortion and the cycle of humiliation reproduces itself as a process of "rotating paranoia." By this I mean that each cell within the distorted system or distorted nexus of human interaction—and by "cell" I mean each individual person as an existing Someone and each artificial "collective" of such persons, like "the Muslim people" or "the American people"—finds its inherent social-spiritual longing for love, recognition, and peace repeatedly short-circuited by a paranoiac fear of the other, a fear that in any situation as complex as the current one has a long and patterned history of precisely this process, evolving pathologically like a single injured organism. On the hopeful side, we must always remember that the social-spiritual longing for love and mutual recognition is "fundamental" while fear and paranoia are not, but are rather derivative of the desire for love and recognition, expressions of the alienation of the fundamental loving desire from itself.

Thus as we analyze the current world situation in 2003 and try to find a new spiritual-political way out of it, we must keenly attune ourselves to this underlying dynamic and its inherently contradictory flow. This attunement of our thinking, this "thinking with the heart," must occur beneath the public clamor—beneath the paranoia-induction of repetitions of certain key names like Saddam Hussein, or George Bush for that matter, which freeze our attunement with a touch of terror, carrying as they do connotations of paranoia, fear, and rage. To heal the world requires thinking, and then gradually acting, underneath this surface of the world and with a single aim: to strengthen the confidence of the longing for love and recognition as it exists across the psycho-spiritual energy field that is the interconnectedness of social space. Like the movement of paranoia and fear, this strengthening also rotates, and through this rotation elevates *itself* into existence. But because of the long history and internalization of the fear that contains it, this process of rotating elevation requires our conscious assistance.

This brings us to the meaning of a new spiritual-political foreign policy. Healing the paranoiac impulse that leads to periodic outbreaks of war, violence, and killing requires an intentional process that I will call "Surrounding." "Surrounding" describes an international, transpersonal effort by the world community to simultaneously contain and reassure the herky-jerky impulse toward fear that irrationally escalates all conflict—that is, it requires both firmness in the sense that is not permissive toward violence in the other, and love in the sense that it manifests, in its very way of being-toward-the-other, a recognition of the other's authentic humanity, even as the other resists that very recognition by throwing up a defensive wall of paranoia and engages in denunciatory words and actions toward the surrounding force.

Surrounding requires that we put up a kind of Guard-all shield that is as impervious as possible to the other's denunciations, that understands they are but expressions of an individual or collective terror and anticipation of humiliation in the other. This shield provides the basis for international empathic firmness, in which love and the capacity to recognize the other holds its ground in spite of accusations and threats. This firmness is actually reassuring to the other that our capacity for recognition is real and unshakeable, that we will not dissolve into counter-violence because of paranoiac shocks leveled in our direction.

The second moment of surrounding then requires the continuing manifestation of recognition of the other's innocent authenticity and constitutes an appeal to the other's longing for recognition and affirmation, seeking to "thaw" the other's paranoia through an insistence on the real existence of the deeper inter-human bond that connects us. We must show through the quality and content of our words and actions that we understand the wounds of the past that we have mostly inherited and partly inflicted on each other—or to be more precise on our singular self-otherness or intersubjectivity—in our own lifetimes, that these wounds are mistakes, that beneath them is a longing for healing and mutual recognition, and that we no longer have any choice but to take the great opportunity forced upon us by the circumstances of modern weaponry and ecological emergency to evolve as a species and transcend the ontological immaturity that has characterized our collective existence up to the present time. This second moment of surrounding is best understood as a manifestation of presence that emanates outward toward the other and recognizes the other in his/her "singular universality" or unique sameness—our very selves in another form.

Surrounding, empathic firmness, thawing by manifesting presence—these are new concepts to us. They can of course be dismissed as New-Age psychobabble by our fearful inherited self-consciousness. But they are qualitative concepts meant to evoke aspects of our social being that, as I have said, exist underneath the world's noisy surface and "subtend" the entire nexus of our collective social reality. This sub-reality is both spiritual and political—spiritual in the sense that it exists pre-verbally in the interspace that irrevocably connects us as inter-subjective social beings; political in the sense that as surely as the need for food and shelter, it drives the way we co-create and govern our collective existence. Everything in human experience is spiritual/political in this sense: A line of people waiting for a bus—to use a famous example of Jean-Paul Sartre's—is spiritual in the sense that in modern society it *exists itself* as a cautious manifestation of rotating anonymity; and political in the sense that it is chosen by "the people" in the line as their way of being together as a collective "no one," drawn from other infinite examples of bus lines and "lines" in general as we form them in a world of social alienation, or rather in a world where social alienation appears to have the upper hand.

But how might this international spiritual/political consciousness express itself? The first part of the answer is for us to realize that in spite of our lack of a vocabulary for it, it already has been expressing itself, in many forms, but especially through the institution of the United Nations. The United Nations is *not* only a collection of States impotently squabbling over this or that international issue without any genuine authority or power in the shadow of Real nation-states that command powerful and deadly militaries and are more or less free to act in their own self-interest. The United Nations is *also* an actual manifestation of the effort of the voice that I here speak of to manifest itself as the Unity of all Being, and to insist that we exist as this unity, and as the collective longing of our desire to affirm this unity. The expression "the Unity of all Being," which Michael Lerner appeals to so often, and which is so difficult to understand and act upon when we are constrained by our dominant secular mindset, expresses the beautiful and true Kabbalistic metaphor that we are but shattered shards of light seeking to recover our awareness of our "singular universality"—that is, our ontological truth that we exist as at once unique in our respective existences and yet manifestations of precisely the same spiritual essence, an essence that can recognize itself through love alone and that longs to recover the capacity for this recognition.

The Charter of the United Nations does not begin with the words, "We, the permanently squabbling and self-interested sovereign States of the world, form ourselves into a sort of pseudo-communal but actually alienated confederation of world nations with no real power, to accomplish little or nothing by diplomatic means, leaving the fate of the earth to the reality of hopelessly divided national self-interests." It begins by affirming in secular language the aspiration of man and womankind toward the recovery of the Unity of all Being through the healing of our differences. And even granting cynical realism its due, it is important and helpful to understand that these high spiritual-political ideals of the Charter were at the time of their expression, following the utter catastrophes of World Wars I and II, genuinely intended by the Charter's signatories to carry this high meaning. If our pre-verbal hopeful longing and even conviction that we are capable in our very nature of universal love and mutual recognition, our knowledge that we are all One, unique and yet the Same, if this longing for recognition did not exist, or if it were untrue, we would have annihilated ourselves long ago. Nations would have annihilated nations as surely as our neighbor would have annihilated his brother-in-law. But just as our knowledge of our interconnectedness and our longing to recognize and affirm it underlies the noise of every event, so also this sense of our co-presence, common desire, and longing partially constitutes our institutions, most nobly the United Nations.

What we might call our theoretical challenge at the present moment is to develop the language and intonation of thinking that can make this spiritual-political conception of an institution like the United Nations explicit and accessible to our common reflection. We must in a certain sense abandon or play down the internalized model that we have of the United Nations as a collection of nation-states—which reflects back to us a picture of a thing-like "entity" made up of various parts, each with its own constituency and interests—and conceive of the UN instead as the embodiment of a world-wide spiritual-political movement toward the mutual recognition of our unity. This new conception, if we are able to allow ourselves to imagine it, should grasp interventions as efforts at healing both the other and ourselves. How, you may ask, can this possibly be relevant to a crisis like that in Iraq, in which—even assuming the totality of present circumstances are reflective of a historical distortion of self-other and inter-cultural relations—we are dealing with very dangerous nuclear, biological, and chemical weapons? At the time of this writing, it may be the case, for example, that Iraq has not accounted for large quantities of anthrax, nerve gas, and possibly significant quantities of pirated or purchased uranium that are in fact capable of killing large numbers of people. Putting aside all the other seemingly overwhelming issues shaping the present situation—including globalization and its impact on the region, the Israeli/Palestinian conflict, the presence of real economic interests that influence the material quality of life of millions of people, and the allegiances of each so-called "nationality" to its own interests and respective collective identity—putting all these and all other "realistic" matters aside, how can one hope by use of a spiritualized perspective to address the dangers of proliferation of weapons of mass destruction and the degree of real danger to millions of lives that these weapons pose?

The answer to this question is that pre-verbal and non-cognitive attempts to Surround even dictators like Saddam Hussein in the manner that I am suggesting will dramatically alter even his desire to use such weapons if he has them—in part by affecting him and those around him, in part by enabling the masses of the Muslim world to feel recognized sufficiently to not support his use of these weapons and instead to try to move toward greater understanding with the real people his actions would affect. Had this approach been taken prior to the current war, we would not be seeing the enraged demonstrations in Yemen now that make the proliferation and use of these weapons more likely, and that once again rotate the paranoiac view of the other that blocks and keeps blocking the other's instinctive movement toward connection. Surrounding, thawing, manifesting Presence, "leaning in" toward the other in a firm but affirming-of-the-other's-humanity way, will *spontaneously* release the other's desire for mutual recognition. This is because the underlying desire of all living beings is for precisely this recognition, and thus this desire responds spontaneously and pre-verbally, like an invisible pre-cognitive force.

Indeed, the discourse of present-day diplomacy, which is not a spiritual discourse, nevertheless makes implicit reference to this spontaneous capacity whenever it speaks of "easing tensions" or of instituting "confidence-building measures." *That which is eased* is the separation from the other, resulting from the legacy of paranoia which in each specific instance takes an historically specific form (Ireland/Britain is different from Israel/Palestine is different from US/Iraq—but not ontologically; rather only in terms of historical and cultural specificity of the respective forms of life that have shaped the historically specific identity of each conflict). The *confidence* that is built in "confidence-building measures" is the commitment to recognition of the other as equal manifestation of the self, achieved through inter-cultural symbolic actions through which mutual recognition is understood to have taken place.

Of course, to repeat what I said earlier, the capacity of healing interventions to produce the spontaneous realization of desire requires symbolic action sufficiently sustained to endure all manner of paranoiac suspicion and counter-reaction. It must be firm enough to endure cynicism and mistrust of every gesture—firm enough to endure the cynicism of the noise at the surface (such as media cynicism) that, because of the legacy of distortion that has produced the conviction that the other will reject the self and vice-versa, and even attempt to exterminate the respective existence of the other, will bombard every act that manifests a healing and loving presence. But our becoming able to "totalize" exactly these processes of mutuality in light of the distortions of our common history is what I mean by spiritualizing foreign policy.

Two recent examples in which this spiritualizing consciousness has had a dramatic effect, and that we can use as models as we try to imagine ourselves lifting out of war-consciousness, are the 1993 Oslo Accords—the most optimistic moment in the history of Israel/Palestinian relations in which each in principle agreed to recognize the other; and South Africa's Truth and Reconciliation Commission—in which the two nations of South Africa, one white and one black, sought to achieve this same mutual recognition in facing and beginning to heal an extraordinarily brutal history of domination of one by the other. From each example, we can learn how to begin to proceed down a new path, focusing our attention on methods of alleviating the stress of paranoia toward the other so that the desire for mutual recognition can emerge, *as it already wishes to do*. From each, we can develop our thought about how to make interventions in the present world situation in which the "we" that is our common humanity can Surround our terror and rage at each other, thaw the frozen rotating paranoia of our mutual antagonisms that have broken us apart, and manifest our presence so as to move toward the peaceful existence to which all living beings aspire.

Prior to the extraordinary "breakfast diplomacy" of Oslo, the Israeli/Palestinian slice of our common humanity sat facing each other across various international tables for four decades. Each having traumatized the other, periodically through physical violence, continually through the humiliation of non-recognition of the humanity of the other, each "side" approached the other as an agent of physical and psycho-spiritual terror. From within this wary and defensive stance, no progress could be made toward peace because true recognition of the other implied a vulnerability on the part of the self that, if not reciprocated, appeared to make the self vulnerable to psychic and perhaps physical annihilation. It is not possible to proceed toward peace in a fixed state of fracture, with the legacy of the Holocaust on one side and the imperialist occupation of the Arab world on the other, from a stance of "you go first," accompanied by a list of demands that are degrading or threatening to the other side.

In the face of that and for a complex of other reasons, in 1993 some Israelis close to then Prime Minister Yitzak Rabin contacted Palestinian leaders close to Yassir Arafat and through a series of miracles agreed to meet in secret in Oslo, Norway, a locale that symbolized a long history of neutrality and far from the spiritual battleground of the Middle East. Under the auspices of their Norwegian hosts, the two sides met not to "negotiate" from a position of mistrust, but to talk and to walk in the green woods of Norway. Relieved of paranoiac pressure in this symbolically neutral setting, the actual persons then engaged in conversations over breakfast in which each for the first time had the opportunity to safely tell the other their story as they experienced it. And precisely because of the locale, the unofficial nature of the dialogue, the fact that it took place while sharing food in a natural surrounding, and the fact that it involved not "goals" and demands to be achieved by rationalistic and strategic conversation, but stories that revealed each side's common humanity, an extraordinary breakthrough was achieved that led to the now famous Oslo Accords, the handshake between former General and hawk Rabin and PLO fighter Arafat in front of Bill Clinton in Washington, D.C., and the very brief outpouring of hope that culminated tragically in Rabin's assassination by a rightwing Jewish settler after a peace rally in which Rabin was seen singing "Give Peace a Chance" with thousands of hopeful young Jews.

I know perfectly well that the line I have drawn here, from the initiation of Oslo to the peace rally at which Rabin was assassinated, and marking the end of that hopeful period, was not in literal, temporal reality a straight line, and also that there is more than one cynical version of the story of Oslo and its meaning. But the so-called "actual facts" as understood by the realists' afterthought misses the point that what I have drawn here was a spiritual straight line, and one that might have led in a very different direction from the present tragic situation. Hunkered down in the legacy of skepticism and pain, realism can never quite see the nonlinear and a temporal openings-up of desire that produce the straight lines of hope in history. Nevertheless, these lines of hope remain lodged, invisible, in our historical memory and silently move the human spirit forward in spite of itself, precisely because they hold the promise of fulfilling the most essential of longings that we universally share.

The key task for us now is to reflect upon these lines of hope as they emerge and gain the knowledge *in our common conscious reflection* of the elements that make the development of hope possible. From Oslo, we can learn elements about time and place, about the role of informality and breaking bread, and about the capacity to tell one's painful story in an environment in which those whom we fear can hear that pain and ultimately identify with it. In that moment of identification comes the possibility of recognition that we *are* the other and that our humanity is not inherently fractured but common; that the other, through mutual recognition, is the source of our own completion as inherently loving, social beings.

The example of South Africa provides a parallel lesson. When Nelson Mandela was in prison, he wrote that he survived his twenty-seven years there in significant part by realizing even in momentary interactions with his guards the essential goodness and humanity that resided within them. This confirmed his conviction that transcendence of even the most brutal history of domination was possible— that this transcendence in some way actually sought its own release from the compulsion to repeat its own repression through domination. When he was finally released and he and Archbishop Desmond Tutu led the overcoming of apartheid, it was this conviction that gave birth to the Truth and Reconciliation Commission, one of the great leaps forward in legal consciousness that has occurred in the development of human history. As is now well-known, this process, in which some 22,000 acts of apartheid-inspired cruelty were acknowledged by the (mainly) white minority perpetrators in the presence of their black victims and their families, on a daily basis and on television for all to hear across the new democratic nation of South Africa, allowed the black majority to assume power essentially without violence and retribution. If one watches the recorded proceedings of this Commission, presided over by the extraordinary moral presence of Bishop Tutu himself, one sees the healing power of the simple speaking of truth to achieve reconciliation and break the cycle of brutality that repeats itself because the pain and suffering beneath it normally cannot be spoken without resulting in what we imagine will produce devastating guilt and humiliation.

Unlike the death penalty, which seeks to provide resolution to the suffering of victims by extermination of the dominating other, the Truth and Reconciliation Commission provided a sufficient beginning toward the resolution of a history of suffering by the act of mass acknowledgment, in which the particular perpetrators were in reality revealing the alienation of the entire white minority that had underlain the essence of apartheid domination and the legacy of imperialism and racism that had given rise to it. The blank statements made by this white landowner or that white policeman—blank because their confessions were often expressed without emotion as a kind of stark and factual representation of a collective truth—placed before the world its own madness, in a way that was simultaneously both monotonously repetitious and spellbinding. And instead of enacting a repetition of the cycle of violence resulting from a repetition of a denial of our common humanity, the processes of the Truth and Reconciliation Commission somehow allowed enactment to be transcended by the naming of the truth that was being denied, in which Tutu himself, as well as the victims and their families themselves, could liberate the nation by bearing witness to it.

Here again, there are many reservations one can raise about the Commission's work, but as in the case of Oslo, the reservations miss the spiritual lesson of how we must proceed to allow ourselves to evolve as an international common humanity, or "international community." On the other side of Truth, of course, is Forgiveness, which is different from freedom from accountability. Bishop Tutu's book *No Future Without Forgiveness* indicates this point in its title—that it is in mutual recognition of the truth of our history, and in forgiveness for this history, which is actually the history of what has been visited upon us as common social individuals in a social/historical common history of humanity, that *spontaneous* redemption becomes possible. I say "spontaneous" redemption because what subtends all of our historical distortions—then apartheid, today Iraq—is the desire for this mutual recognition, the desire to recognize the other and be recognized by the other in a precognitive relation of common presence. That is what heals and what we mean by love.

So now we move to the present crisis. I have said that the UN should re-envision itself according to its original moment of creation, but do so before the catastrophe (that is, the next rotation of paranoia and fear that is already in the process of unfolding) rather than after it. This was the case in 1945 when the Charter was first written and its principles committed to through the act of signature. What follows is a possible spiritual-political path that the UN might have taken prior to this war and could conceivably still take, with the cooperation of the United States, as of the time of this writing.

We must begin from the starting point that the UN exists as an embodiment of common humanity seeking to recognize and return to itself, to get back in touch with its original form and intention, and to redeem itself, through actions that heal the distortions of *itself* that come before it in one particular form after another.

First, the UN Security Council, as a group constituted to be expressive of the world's effort to recognize and affirm our common humanity, should explicitly pass a resolution that reassures the people of Iraq, and the peoples of the Middle East generally, that it does not wish to engage in further acts of violence toward them, but rather seeks to insure their safety and well-being. This resolution should include provisions for significant humanitarian assistance. But in addition, the resolution should make clear *humanity's* common fear of nuclear, biological, and chemical weapons that Iraq and other nations may possess, and invite the existing Iraqi leadership to participate in a mediated dialogue about how systematically to reduce this level of fear. This must include a willingness to address the paranoiac or realistic fears that even Saddam Hussein may hold about the safety of Iraq in the face of Western weaponry, and begin a dialogue about what to do about this fear. Explicit in the design of this dialogue must be the paradox that neither side wishes to disarm in the face of the fear of the other.

One manner of conducting such a dialogue would be to have world leaders who are widely recognized to represent the highest of human ideals, such as Nelson Mandela, Mikail Gorbachev, Jimmy Carter, and Kofi Annan, along with an ecumenical group of leading religious figures, including the Pope, to convene and oversee its deliberations. These deliberations should be at least partially televised, just as the hearings of South Africa's Truth and Reconciliation Commission were, so that the process of dialogue and the emerging process of mutual recognition of one another's humanity that would be intended to emerge from it could be witnessed each day by people throughout the world.

Second, in the conduct of this dialogue, each participant should have an opportunity to state its past wounds, so that without blame, humanity as a whole, as symbolized by the United Nations convening body, could hear the suffering it has imposed upon itself. Here the entire historical legacy of the experience of each party's suffering and humiliation should be given expression—families of Americans who died on September 11 should speak to and be seen by the world via television as speaking to Iraqi families whose children have died as a result of war and economic sanctions. Here, the goal would be for our common humanity to elicit its own spontaneous compassion for the trauma and wounds we have inflicted on ourselves.

You might at first think that it makes little sense for Iraqi families to engage in such a dialogue with American families since Iraq was presumably not responsible for the destruction of the World Trade Center and the deaths of September 11. But understood through a spiritual-political lens, the impetus for war between America and Iraq emerges from the interrelationship of traumatic, paranoia-inducing events and histories that are expressive of each group's projection of the other as a projected agent of terror and humiliation. Expression of the experience of suffering by members of each group in a publicly televised forum, heard with compassion by the symbol of the world community manifesting its presiding presence, listening to the effects of its own distortions, is one of the most powerful ways of "thawing" the carapace of pseudo-identities that keep us locked in the rotating paranoia of the war paradigm. Through the presence of the suffering of the other, we "hear" through the pain of identification how out of touch we are with ourselves, how split from the unity of our oneness and commonality.

Third, the UN should seek to "invite," perhaps within the circular arena of the Security Council, a mutual embrace or other expression of mutual recognition between families and across nationalistic pseudo-identities, taking care that this is done authentically. If we remember that the desire for mutual recognition of our common humanity—at the level of the people in our families or in the buildings in which we live as much as at the international level—always subtends the rotating paranoia that separates us, and that this desire for connection is capable of spontaneous emergence (think of the elevated local and world responses in the first two weeks following September 11), it is clear that a spiritual foreign policy must be one that utilizes mass communication technologies to permit the witnessing of such spontaneous emergence. Quiet the voice that might lead you to think this is a crazy idea, that it is inconceivable or otherwise "unrealistic": Israeli peace activist Yitzak Frankenthal's "Parents Circle–Families Forum" has already enabled such public acts of embrace and reconciliation to occur between victims of terror and occupation in Israel/Palestine, and there is no reason why the Security Council could not reimagine its work to emphasize public actions necessary for healing that take account of Frankenthal's proven spiritual wisdom.

If an embrace between families is not possible or capable of being realized with authentic spontaneity in the context of a public hearing, the presence of this hesitancy can be valuable in itself. Merely listening, through the medium of specific actors understood as injured and scattered shards of light, to the pain we have inflicted on ourselves through being out-of-touch-with-ourselves, is sufficient to set on course our ethical direction; and if seen through this spiritual-political lens, the incapacity to embrace in response to an invitation to do so points both actor and witness toward the redemptive necessity of engaging in those acts of reconciliation, generosity, and kindness that can allow the desire for such an embrace to manifest itself eventually. It is this recognizing embrace, spontaneously pulled for in and through the suffering we have inflicted on ourselves, that we have withheld across generations because we have remained trapped in reciprocally perceiving and responding to the other as a threat.

Fourth, UN representatives should supplement ordinary humanitarian aid with rebuilding the material infrastructure of the Middle East as a whole where such manifestations of generosity can be carried out, including post-war Iraq, no matter what the swirl of emotions, no matter what the political complexity, that such efforts will encounter. This rebuilding should especially include homes, hospitals, schools, and facilities to ensure safe drinking water and provision of food supplies. But it should also include assistance to local communities in rebuilding mosques and other locations that symbolize the historical embodiment of the region's cultural integrity. The aim here as an expression of Surrounding is to freely link acts of generosity with the transmission of recognition, and to proceed to thaw traumatized areas manifesting resistance toward participation in the activity of our common humanity in recovering contact with, and shared knowledge of, itself.

Finally, all of these activities can and should be replicated by the redemptive movements of our common humanity that exist within an increasing singular and worldwide civil society—that is, redemptive actions outside existing institutions that are already being engaged in by the millions of us whom we know make up the new, worldwide peace (not merely anti-war) movement. We are ordinary people committed to the recovery of our capacity to release the desire to recognize each other as the source of each other's completion. In relation to the spiritual sickness of war-consciousness and the now-ancient paradigm that separates us, we are all doctors without borders. Common humanity can heal itself only by healing the other through providing the other with the grace of a recognition that every one of us longs for through the layer of pain and self-protection that causes us to distort who the other actually is, and withhold ourselves from the only source of our salvation.

ESSAY THIRTEEN

THE FEAR OF GAY MARRIAGE

"It's not who ya love,
It's do ya love"

—Michael Franti, Spearhead

"EVERY MINUTE THEY CONTINUE, THOSE CEREMONIES ARE DESTROYING my relationship with my wife." These words, spoken by one of the men who filed suit to stop San Francisco Mayor Gavin Newsom from issuing marriage licenses to gays and lesbians provide great insight into the psychodynamics underlying the 2004 presidential election. For moral values like the belief in the sanctity of traditional marriage "between one man and one woman" are not abstract beliefs that rattle around in one's head; they are rather powerfully rooted in the desire for human connection, and in the sense-memories that we all have of how we have previously lived out this connection in our sensual lives. When a plaintiff watching gays and lesbians get married on television claims that they are destroying his relationship with his wife, he is telling a truth about his experience—namely, that what he is watching makes him feel he is losing a sense of being connected to another person, that he is hemorrhaging, that he believes that the integrity of his own social existence is somehow being threatened and compromised.

There is a sense in which this person's views are "crazy." He is living in fear that the blessing of erotic love between two persons other than himself can destroy the sense-memory that he has of the possibility of this erotic love for himself. But seen in a wider social context, his craziness may be eminently sane. For if the world around him is profoundly alienated; if he is living in a social environment characterized by mutual distance, detachment, and disconnection; if he is enveloped by deadening routines at work and media images at home that seem to be artificial (commercials), or relentlessly self-mocking (sitcoms), or hostile (MTV), or devoid of meaning (the interchangeable hollowness of "the

131

news"), then he rightly clings to what sense-memories he does have of actually being *with* someone, of not being alone.

This is not to say he actually has this experience in a complete way with his actual wife. If he did, it is very unlikely, and perhaps inconceivable, that he would want to deny this experience to someone else. It is rather that erotic expression as the realization of his longing for social connection is encoded in his memory from early infancy as the sensual holding that he experienced with a mothering one, and that this memory has been elaborated in later years through the whole of his relationship with women, including his wife. The later experience, perhaps supported by the fellow-feeling of the church group and by the positive erotic charge emitted by the evangelical preacher, sustains and is fused with the earlier enfolding experience, the initial laying down of heterosexual safety. In an alienated world in which people feel mainly alone and constantly threatened with an even more devastating isolation, they understandably cling to whatever sense-memories of erotic connection they have, and they guard these memories themselves against the threat of loss that surrounds them.

Indeed one of the problems with heterosexual marriage as an institution is precisely that it sacralizes the separation of the erotic couple from the wider community—it channels the flow of deeply bonding social energy into one single path and thus may contribute to blocking that flow outward toward those whom we encounter everywhere else around us. This isn't to say that people should not hold public ceremonies to affirm their love for one another before and within the whole community. It's rather to say that the embrace of church/state-sponsored marriage to do so is embracing a social institution whose ceremony of vows, sealed with a kiss, does in fact carry with it an erotic history that has separated the couple from the wider community. In Christopher Lasch's famous phrase, the family becomes a "haven in a heartless world," but the world is heartless in part because of the separation of loving energy from it and the pooling up of that energy within the haven itself. In such circumstances, the haven cannot really be a haven any more than one can really chew on an impacted tooth. The erotic isolation of the family may be a cause of domestic violence, but it remains rational for people to cling to it for dear life if the alternative is the panic of a more devastating isolation.

So we must have compassion for those who come out to vote for their own social sanity, even as we throw all the weight of our being in a completely different direction, the direction of an opening up of desire in which we can all affirm and love one another as manifestations of G-d's energy. What we must find a way to do, and what we must encourage liberal/left leaders post-John Kerry who are trying to speak for all of us in public space to do, is to extend ourselves toward the other in a way that recognizes and affirms his/her deepest longings, that says, "Yes, I feel this too. It's right to feel it. It's not terrifying to feel it. Nothing will be destroyed if you feel it. And here is how we are going to *realize* this divine and common longing in our flesh-and-blood social existence." I'm not speaking here about non-monogamy; I'm speaking about, say, universal health care, but universal health care as expressive of our devotion to each other's well-being and our deep concern for one another's families, and not a dully articulated, emptied-of-meaning slogan thrown into a laundry list of other slogans and rattled out in a stump speech or in a party platform. It means calling for universal health care as an expression of actually caring for each other's health, rather than simply advocating for a third-party to insure each other's bodies.

The Democrats lost in 2004 because they still, after thirty years of looking, cannot find their erotic voice—the voice that they once had as compassionate and caring spokespersons for the New Deal and as morally compelling advocates for the Civil Rights movement. But the way for us to help the Democrats or any other political group that can help to move us forward is not to wait for them to awaken to the spiritual and erotic dimensions of politics, but to do what we can to awaken to that dimension in ourselves. For insofar as politics is a preverbal erotic energy flow that sparks social hope and out of that energy finds the words for evoking our common aspirations for a life-affirming moral community, the social ground and origin for such a politics just has to begin within ourselves, in a "parallel universe" that is independent of the artificial role-playing and pseudo-humanity that comprise so much of mainstream public life. Let us take the opportunity of this thoroughgoing 2004 electoral defeat to pull back out of the "what will the Democrats do next?" mentality and into a search for our own most authentic moral convictions that aim for our highest ideals. It is by confirming these authentic ideals in each other, through group experiences like participation in the Network of Spiritual Progressives chapters or in our synagogues, union halls, and other spiritual-political activities located outside the official realms of blocked connection (the corporation, the state, and the media, with the family as a swing space, although no space is ever completely blocked) that we are likely to find each other in a confirming and life-enhancing way and transmit to each other the social confidence that always precedes the outflow of what we call "social movement."

And it is the radiation of this energy outward from its own center, from our own center, that will influence candidates, legislators, judges, the political parties. For these public actors, as for the evangelicals who think that their own social well-being requires the banning of others' social well-being, it is the radiance of confident love turned outward that will eventually heal the fear of love.

ESSAY FOURTEEN

A CALL FOR SACRED BIOLOGISTS

IF "THE EVOLUTION OF SPECIES IS THE GREATEST SACRED DRAMA OF ALL TIME," as Art Green claims in his beautiful essay "Sacred Evolution" (*Tikkun*, Mar/Apr 2010), then we need sacred biologists to help us witness and interpret it.

We can certainly appreciate Charles Darwin for his insight into the existence of evolution, but we must also recognize how much his view of the evolutionary process itself was cramped by the so-called "scientific method" and its despiritualized way of apprehending the world. The scientific method seeks its limited truths by standing back from phenomena and grasping the world "objectively" through what it imagines to be neutral observation, but what is in reality a biased way of looking at things with an eye devoid of spirit. Thus it was understandable that Darwin, as a practitioner of this method, would conceive that evolution could be explained by natural selection—by the idea that the species evolve through accidental adaptive changes from a common ancestor, changes across generations that favor the material fact of survival. If there is more going on—for example, a sacred drama in which Being is seeking to make itself manifest through love incarnated through potentially infinite historical forms—Darwin would not have been able to see it. His neutral observation rendered the spiritual dimension invisible because it neutralized the "living things" he observed.

Natural selection is certainly part of the story—namely, the part that pertains to mere material survival in the face of transformations in climatic and other material conditions. But if we understand the radiance of life as Art Green does, we must newly attend to the Being of plants and animals, to the extraordinary unfolding of their interior presence manifested across the generations, to the meaning of the plant's branches outstretched toward the sun, to the meaning of the panda's long and eventually successful struggle to grip bamboo with an opposable thumb, and to the meaning of the emergence of self-consciousness in humans like ourselves as an upward movement of historical awareness, of Being itself becoming aware of itself. To say it's all natural selection in the service of survival is analogous to

Bill Clinton and now perhaps Barack Obama believing that "it's the economy, stupid" when it comes to the longings of human beings, who in truth want not merely to survive but to become fully present to each other through love and recognition. It's a way of seeing that fails to apprehend what Teilhard de Chardin called "the within of things," the beautiful effort of the soul to manifest itself more and more fully through the unfolding of historical forms.

To understand the sacred drama of the evolutionary process, we need the help of evolutionary biologists who are not neutral observers in the classically liberal sense, but who connect the sacred within themselves to the sacred dimension of what they observe in the natural world. We need biologists who, to use Art Green's words, engage in a "letting go" that allows them to open themselves "with full engagement of the self in love and awe" to the observation and understanding of all animate life, and who understand instinctively that when it comes to scientific research, it is the quality of the awareness in the subject that determines what is visible in the object. These biologists could help us understand why plants share water during droughts (an empirical fact that puzzles materialist science); or how these same plants "lean toward the light" with branches, stems, and leaves stretching toward the sun in a sensual unity that inspires us to water and attend to them in a way that mere "photosynthesis" could never do; or the role of joy in bird flight and in the evolution of the wing (for the sanderling must be able to "whirl" with his community); or the role of love in the development of the kangaroo's pouch.

The point here is that these physical and morphological phenomena that normal science today describes in a largely anatomical and functional way (i.e., that such-and-such trait developed "in the service of survival") in truth occur in a spiritual and social milieu that must be compassionately and lovingly perceived, patiently studied, and evocatively illuminated. Only in this way will the theory of evolution align itself with the truth that spirit and matter form an indissoluble unity, and that we can only be the outcome of the evolutionary process that Darwin says we are if we are related "from the inside," via the "within of things," to the life that preceded and gave birth to us.

ESSAY FIFTEEN

THE PRESENCE OF LIVING ORGANISMS

IN "THE SECRET LIFE OF PLANTS" (*Tikkun*, Nov/Dec 2010), Ray Barglow criticizes my attribution of an in-dwelling presence to plant life by saying, essentially, that my attribution is wrong because science has demonstrated that the movement of plants can be explained by purely material factors. He cites a passage in which I appeal to the reader to agree that when plants turn toward the light, we sense their presence as living beings. Barglow rejects my appeal, saying that scientists have shown that "hormones" called "auxins" cause this turning, by stimulating cell division on the shady side of the plant, causing the plant to bend away from the shady section and toward the light.

But if we look more carefully at the way the scientist develops his or her knowledge about auxins, we can see that the scientist has simply *redescribed* the plant's behavior solely in terms of the plant's material elements. The scientist first looks at the plant as an "object," then takes note of the behavioral fact that the plant bends toward the light, then examines biochemical processes that are visible under a microscope that accompany this bending, and then invents certain concepts to name the biochemical elements in the plant that make the bending possible (in this case, the scientist uses the Greek-derived concept "hormone," meaning "stimulate," and the similarly Greek-derived concept "auxin," meaning "grow," to describe the empirically observed gooey stuff that appears to be associated with increased cell division in the plant). The scientist has not by this process explained what causes the plant perceived as an object to bend; he or she has simply redescribed the bending process itself in terms of the visible, material processes that are associated with the bending.

The great error of "scientism," as we refer to it in *Tikkun*, is to mistake this material redescription for an explanation. Since the scientist may believe, as a matter of conviction, that all that can be said to be "real" is what is visible to the objectifying, detached gaze, the scientist may a) notice the plant's bending behavior in the presence of sunlight; b) invent certain concepts like auxins to describe the biochemical correlates of the behavior; c) "reify" the concepts, meaning treat the gooey stuff he or she has named "auxin" as if it were a real thing called auxin; and d) assume that this production of auxin is the "true cause" that explains the bending behavior. He or she may assume—"Well, there's nothing else going on that we can see."

I acknowledge that it is possible that there is "nothing going on" except a mere physical process—that sunlight stimulates the tip of a plant to spur the production of auxins that cause the plant to bend. But it is also possible that the plant as a living and vital presence responds to the warmth and radiance of the sunlight and turns toward it responsively, with the production of auxins being merely the biochemical, material correlate of that turning process. This latter interpretation, which I favor, understands the plant as a spiritual-material unity rather than reducing the plant to the materialist dimension that is visible to the detached, scientific eye. To see the spiritual element requires that we trust our intuitive response to the plant's outreaching tendrils, that we "let ourselves go toward the plant" rather than "standing back" and looking "at" it. I say to the scientist: "If you let go of your standing back and if you instead 'go forward,' and if you then spontaneously sense the plant's responsiveness to the sun, you will see it is reaching toward the sunlight, and you have helpfully showed the material means, the biochemical correlative process, by which it has enabled itself to do this. Amazing!"

By "standing back" I do not mean that biologists are detached people or that they don't greatly appreciate nature. I know lots of them do and that's why they become interested in the natural world. By "detachment" or "standing back" I'm referring to the epistemological stance of empiricism itself, a detachment that is the very basis of its claim to objectivity and neutrality as regards its own conception of "validity." I'm saying as long as you take that stance, you can't perceive the spiritual/invisible dimension of the world. On the other hand, when you "go forward" or let go of that neutral di-stance, you become one with the spiritual dimension, a spiritual dimension that is actually self-evident to the engaged intuition that comprehends life moment to moment. I'm also claiming that that engaged intuition can approach its own objectivity through communal discourse and reflection, in a way that's analogous to but yet completely different from the natural science method—namely, by serious reflective discussion in a peer community in which intuitively grounded perceptions are tested discursively and corrected for biases such as anthropomorphism, projection, and other common interpretive distortions.

But please note that I am not merely saying that the spiritual way of seeing exists alongside the scientific way. Rather, I am saying that the spiritual dimension—the dimension of the life-world accessible to intuition—is the ontological ground of the total epistemological enterprise. This ground is Being itself, and to "know" the life-world, the knower must travel a pathway from one's own interior to the interior of the known. One must "go forward" via intuition and empathy into the heart of the known, which is composed of the same Being, the knower's own Being.

For specific purposes, the knower may make use of an ingenious special practice that we now call the scientific method, with its techniques of detachment, objectification of phenomena, correlation of sense data, experimentation including altering of material conditions, and the formulation and testing of hypotheses. This specialized practice produces information that may be useful and "valid" according to its own terms but is not true in an ontological sense, nor does it aspire to truth in this sense. There is a possibility that what we now call inanimate matter is in reality just dead, inert matter, in which case the existing disciplines of physics and inorganic chemistry might actually be producing truth because there may be no ontological commonality between the knower and the known, and the known may in fact be nothing but a passive material object, although this is doubtful considering the vitality of what we call energy and the relationship of mass to energy. But as regards animate matter, the use of what I'm calling the scientific method can produce no more than provisional verification of hypotheses pertaining to the known phenomenon when we pretend that the phenomenon is a mere object—when we treat it as if it were an object for some useful purpose. It can't be "true" in an ontological sense because an animate phenomenon *exists*, is *alive*, is a portion of the Being of the knower, or better, a manifestation of it.

In the context of evolutionary theory, the scientific determination to exclude the "invisible" from what is "real" has led to an unfortunate aspiration to explain the entire unfolding and development of life by the "standing back" approach. Like my plant scientist, the evolutionary biologist seems to want to "stand back" from the fossil record, examine parts of objectified bodies as they change over time, and then invent a concept that can explain the entire process without recourse to anything "invisible." The main explanatory concept since Darwin has been "natural selection." By "standing back" the scientist can "observe" that some plants and animals have survived and others have not, that adaptive changes have facilitated survival, and since no other mechanisms of evolutionary progress that satisfy the requirements of "visibility" have been sufficiently supported by empirical evidence, the scientist proposes that natural selection explains all of evolution. With the growth and development of the science of genetics, adaptive changes themselves have come to be explained by genetic mutations that are presumed to occur randomly and accidentally (a purposeful alteration would depend on an "invisible" influence that the "standing back" method has declared to be nonexistent, or at least unknowable).

As in the case of the plant scientist interpreting plants' turning toward sunlight, the Darwinian evolutionary biologist uses the "standing back" method of looking to develop very useful and helpful-to-humankind knowledge about the material world—in this case identifying the very existence of evolution itself—but then goes too far and allows his or her method of looking to box him/her in to a closed and self-referential explanatory narrative that is a matter of belief rather than proof or demonstration. By adhering to the a priori conviction or belief that only what is visible to the standing-back eye, the detached eye, is real, the biologist locks him/herself into an explanatory hypothesis that says: "All that is visible is survival. Therefore accidental adaptation furthering survival is all there is."

Here are four problems with this proposal:

1. It suggests that the vast unfolding of life across time and through the extraordinary manifestations of the various species of plants and animals can be accounted for by a single, essentially passive factor: survival. It declares a priori based on the "visibility-to-the-detached-eye" requirement that there is no interiority or forward motion to the ascension from microscopic bacteria to human life.

2. Because the natural sciences method excludes all but the empirically visible— because it erases by epistemological fiat the influence of Being or Spirit on the evolutionary process—the theory of natural selection can be entirely correct on its own terms and yet be false in relation to reality. The fact that evolution *can* be explained by natural selection does not mean that it *is* explained by natural selection, and even if there were a perfect fit between the hypothesis of natural selection and the empirical data provided by the fossil record and other sources, that would only make the theory the more deceptive if the excluded aspect of reality, the spiritual dimension, is in truth at the heart of the matter.

3. As Christian de Quincey emphasizes in "Nature Has a Mind of Its Own" (*Tikkun*, Nov/Dec 2010), the theory of natural selection simply cannot account for the appearance of consciousness or the evolution of consciousness because to call consciousness an accidental adaptation in the service of survival suggests that non-conscious matter could somehow, by an accidental mutation, make an ontological "leap" into becoming sentient, then conscious, then conscious of itself.

4. Even apart from the problem of accounting for the appearance of consciousness, because of the visibility-to-the-detached-eye requirement, the theory of natural selection and all other materialist theories of evolution reduce the totality of the evolution of existence to its objectified physical manifestations.

This means that as I, a sixty-three-year-old man typing on a computer in the year 2010, sit here and think about the prevailing natural-selection theory of evolution from microorganisms to me, there is no possibility of any interior, existential relationship between me as an actual living person and all the life-forms that have preceded me and that have been evolving "toward" me. By an unconscious trick inhering in the method itself, inherent in the visibility-to-the-detached-eye requirement, the evolutionary biologist has both erased his own existence as a living existential being from the evolutionary process and "canceled out" the Being of everything in the entire upward movement of the evolutionary enterprise. To put this another way, Mr. Darwin is not *in* his own theory and neither is any *one* else. As the Talking Heads put it, "lights on, nobody home."

What I am proposing is not that we reject the contributions of Charles Darwin or of the great naturalist field of evolutionary biology, but that we open ourselves to the possibility that Darwin and his successors have made an error in radically separating spirit (or consciousness) from matter and that we must take a new approach if we are to grasp the spiritual-material unity of the life-world in its true unfolding through its manifestations in plant, animal, and human life. This requires that we adopt a new method of gaining knowledge based upon a new conception of the Being of living manifestations (there are no "living things"). This we do by beginning with our own Being as living presences inhabiting and co-constituting a meaningful life-world suffused with desire and intention, including both material projects (the desire not merely to survive but to achieve full vitality or health) and inter-subjective social projects (the desire to give and receive nurturance and love, to complete ourselves through transparent mutual recognition, to together transcend ourselves toward some ultimate unity or Oneness). Beginning with the recognition of this spiritual essence at the heart of his or her own Being, the scientist then must "go forward and comprehend" rather than only "stand back and observe"; he or she must embrace the teeming life-world as a universal spiritual presence manifested uniquely in every embodied living organism. The central medium of investigation in this approach to the pursuit of knowledge is not detached analysis of empirically visible sense data, but rather intuition of meaningful manifestations of embodied social consciousness. In other words, we must anchor ourselves in the self-evident knowledge that Being has of its own presence and intentionality, and engage in empathic apprehension of the other forms of life that surround us in our own time, or past forms of life accessible through meaning-revealing artifacts that both point backward toward shaping material and social conditions and forward toward the projects that these earlier life-forms were at their moment on earth seeking to realize. This is the path by which we can come to grasp the evolution of the species as the upward movement of Being that it self-evidently is, worthy of the vast intelligence manifested in every living form and worthy of the immanent bond that unites us to every living form.

PART FOUR

CULTURE

THIS LAST SECTION ON THE SPIRITUAL DIMENSION OF CULTURE shows in four short essays how culture is a moral environment, how cultural creations can either serve to unconsciously foster resignation to a despiritualized world or to unveil the spiritual and moral dimension of the world so as to make the viewer or reader want to transcend its limitations. The rise of postmodernism in the last three decades has prioritized irony as a medium of connection to the other: To take two very popular examples, from the sublime Stephen Colbert to the ridiculous "Two and a Half Men," the rise of irony in both high and low culture has allowed people to escape being totally enclosed within the suffering of the world through sharing the experience of laughing at it, and through that to maintain a quotation-mark detachment from the world's fear, cruelty, and violence. On the one hand, that is better than nothing—it's better to laugh together than to be silenced into submission to what supposedly Is, and I like both Colbert and "Two and a Half Men." On the other hand, irony is flight—it responds to oppression by offering a shared escape that is much too thin a platform from which to launch a movement for transformation.

What culture can be is art or play or simply "manifestation" that affirms the visibility of the invisible, affirms the immanent spiritual longing that exerts a constant, hopeful pressure on the empirical world. Like the speeches of Martin Luther King Jr., whose birthday it is today as I write these words, these creations are founded upon a future conviction that reveals the hope in the present and pulls the viewer or reader in that same moral direction. In the essays that follow, I show this moral potential in four cultural contexts: the work of Jean-Paul Sartre, whose critique of the world as it is relies entirely on an intuition of the possible and necessary transcendence of that world; the world of sports not as mere play, but as a potentially contested moral arena which can valorize militarism and nationalism or advance civic responsibility and social justice; the photography of Robert Bergman as he reveals the face of the other in a way that moves you to want to heal the world; and a description of illness not as diminishment but as potentially transformative vulnerability.

ESSAY SIXTEEN

THE SPIRIT OF SARTRE

TAKEN AS A WHOLE, the work of Jean-Paul Sartre is that of a sensitive man with a good heart gradually coming to understand the distinctly social aspect of human reality—that while we appear to ourselves as alone and struggling to make sense of things from within our own isolation, we are actually always powerfully connected in our very being to each other and, through the networks of reciprocity that enable our material and spiritual survival, to everyone on the planet.

Sartre's early work for which he is best remembered in mainstream liberal culture—the period in his thirties and forties that produced the novel *Nausea*, the philosophical work *Being and Nothingness*, and the plays *The Flies* and *No Exit*, among many, many other writings—were all addressed to "the man alone" struggling to find authentic meaning in a world without God and in a world pervaded by false images and false conceptions of what matters in life. To a young person like me gradually emerging into the radical awareness of the 1960s, this work was thrilling. I was brought up within the image-world of upper-middle-class New York culture, taught by word and gesture to accept that artificial world of the bourgeoisie as if it conformed to some real "essence," as if the right thing to do in life was to do well in school, dress nicely, acquire my share of wealth by entrepreneurship or inheritance, get married, fit well and admirably into this or that pre-given role, and have a solid obituary. But to use the famous phrase drawn from one of his lectures, Sartre showed that "existence precedes essence"—that all of these preconstructed forms of identity, worth, and value were actually made up, that it was "bad faith" to allow our longing for superficial security to rationalize draping them over ourselves as if they would safely install us in some kind of "reality," that we are free to accept or reject every form of received wisdom and, even more, that we are personally responsible to make these choices and by these choices to give our own stamp to reality and take our own stand for all of humankind about the kind of world we ought to be creating.

As important as these insights were—and as empowering as they were to me as a young man trying to find the strength to choose to align myself with the idealistic aspirations of the movements of the sixties and to take the risk of rejecting the class destiny to which I was bound by the erotic ties of family loyalty and devotion—Sartre himself came to realize that they were skewed and limited by the liberal individualism of his own upbringing; these early insights illuminated the world from within the pathos and solitude and psycho-spiritual struggles and relative material privilege of the floating or unanchored bourgeois intellectual. Thus his early philosophical understanding of "Relations with Others," as elaborated in *Being and Nothingness* and in his early plays, reflected the fear of the other that he came to see later as the unconscious foundation of "individualism" itself. To the early Sartre, the other is mainly a threat whose gaze "steals my freedom" by pinning me in an image-for-the-other that is colored with pride or shame and from which I must recover myself as a free being through a kind of ontological struggle, a struggle perfectly captured in the famous line from *No Exit*: "Hell is other people." In many ways, as radical as Sartre's early ideas were in rejecting the conformity of inauthentic social life and its mores, roles, and hierarchies, they remained quite consistent with the aspect of liberal Western society that defined "man" as a free being inherently separate from and in conflict with the freedom of the other. This is no doubt one reason that his "existentialism" is today taught in every liberal university while his later conversion to Marxism and social commitment and his brilliant reconciliation of the insights of existentialism with those of Marxism are almost nowhere to be studied and learned.

That later integration began to take place when Sartre served in the French army in World War II: through his conscription he began to grasp that he was involuntarily bound to others by social forces much larger than the mainly two-person interactions that he was in those very years exploring in his philosophy; and his deepening awareness of the inherently social nature of each individual's existence was accelerated by the encounter that every serious intellectual had with Marxism and its "really existing" embodiment in the Soviet Union following World War II. But in spite of the sympathy that Sartre had for the Soviet Union's egalitarian ideal in the face of McCarthyism and the increasingly reactionary cast of Western capitalism in the early 1950s, he knew that the Soviet Union was a grossly distorted manifestation of Marxist ideals and that its distortions were in no small part the result of the limitations of the state of Marxist theory itself— indeed, of its very failure to give sufficient ontological priority to the subjective, qualitative experience of actual human relations that was the central concern of his own work. Thus he felt it fell to him as a kind of moral responsibility to throw himself into showing how Marxism had become false to its own human aspirations by the hyper-objectivity of its own pseudo-scientific theory, how its transformation from a culturally complex and human historical materialism into a mechanistic and externalized "dialectical materialism" had led it to rationalize a new form of class society and social oppression as if it were a near-messianic embodiment of social progress.

Published in 1960, Sartre's *Critique of Dialectical Reason* was an effort to show that while Marxism was correct in giving primacy to materialism—to the need for food, clothing, and shelter as being the key shaping force that had thus far connected all humans to each other and mediated their relationships to one another in a milieu of material scarcity and the struggle for survival—Marxist thinking nevertheless had to incorporate into itself the relatively independent longing for human freedom and for the transcendence of the intersubjective and distinctively social facts of oppression, exploitation, and alienation of self from other to accurately understand and portray the truth of social life and offer a path to improving it. In this later philosophical work and in his later plays like *The Devil and the Good Lord* and *The Condemned of Altona*, as well as in several volumes of essays and a three-volume biographical study of Flaubert, Sartre replaced his earlier emphasis on the "man alone" struggling for freedom and authenticity with the social individual bound to all living others through the necessities of economic production and bound also to prior generations through the medium of the world of "worked matter" that we have inherited from them and which directs and limits our possible forward motion. In place of the floating and unanchored individual seeking to recover his or her authentic being from the inauthenticity of a fallen society living in bad faith and in flight from itself through a kind of ubiquitous personal and moral inadequacy, Sartre makes a powerful and original argument for a collective, intersubjective, distinctively social recovery of our authentic human capacities, a recovery achievable through the "praxis" of collective action to transcend class society and the alienating reciprocal conditioning through which we have enslaved ourselves and each other to dehumanizing socio-economic forces over which no one has control.

John Gerassi's 2009 book *Talking with Sartre* is a transcription of a fascinating series of interviews conducted with Sartre by Gerassi over the period from 1970–1974, just as Sartre himself was coming to question whether his own later theory of existential Marxism was adequate to either offer a new path to human liberation for the Left or account for the extraordinary dynamics that had been sweeping the world in the form of "the sixties" during the previous decade. Gerassi, the son of longtime family friends of Sartre and Simone de Beauvoir and already an established independent left intellectual in his early forties at the time of these interviews, serves as a comradely inquisitor of Sartre as the great philosopher was approaching his seventieth birthday and could not but see the shortcomings of the social movements of the sixties beginning to manifest themselves in historically decisive ways. The interviews are in a certain sense a first-person evaluation of the state of the Left worldwide, as they reflect Sartre's thoughts on his own visits to the Soviet Union, Mao's China, and Castro's Cuba, as well as his own participation in the radical groups in France—in particular the *gauche prolétarienne* and its newspaper, *La Cause du Peuple*, of which Sartre had become the editor.

To those who today are working toward the creation of a spiritual-political progressive movement, the most important sections of the book deal with Sartre's evaluation of his own ideas about how we are to overcome the social alienation that at the time of these interviews and still today seems to separate us from each other and disable us from banding together to create a more loving, egalitarian, solidaristic world. In the *Critique of Dialectical Reason*, Sartre had developed two important ideas that remain relevant to us today as we try to build a new movement and understand the psychosocial dynamics that inhibit our efforts. One is the idea of "seriality"—the idea that when we are thrown by socioeconomic forces into relationships based on competition for survival and are conditioned by the weight of historical traditions and social ideologies to accept our situation as necessary and even desirable, we each become stuck in a kind of social quicksand in which other people seem to be constantly receding away from us like threads in an inside-out shirt and in which we ourselves each become "one of the others" to each receding other, collectively casting one another into a mutually distancing, one-and-one separation that we can't seem to get out of. Whether we are languishing in the passive rituals of family life, or passing each other with blank gazes on the street, or carrying out the repetitive routines of work in offices or on assembly lines, when we are trapped in the one-and-one series, we exist as passive occupiers of social slots without a common active or creative purpose that unites us in any sort of original collective project: we cannot seem to translate our longing for vitalizing social connection into any form of meaningful action that would allow us to recover our spontaneity and freedom. A key question for Sartre in the *Critique* had been what form of collective action could enable us to lift ourselves out of this self-reproducing separation that actually was the central dynamic reproducing capitalism itself, an anti-human system that we all feel trapped in as if it were coming from "outside" us, like a nonhuman force over which we have no control.

Sartre's answer to this question in the *Critique* had been that under certain favorable conditions combining the right material circumstances with the right spark of cultural (or countercultural) inspiration and also the irreducible power of human freedom exerting itself against its own self-reproducing constraints, human beings could break through the reciprocal imprisonment of the series to form what he called "the fused group"—a movement toward mutual freedom and solidarity that would overwhelm the external conditioning that renders us passive, atomized, anonymous (in the sense of lacking in authentic presence and lost in robotic roles and routines), and interchangeable. Drawing on the inspiration of revolutionary historical moments such as the seizures of the Bastille and the Winter Palace, the rebellion of the Kronstadt sailors, and the spontaneous sit-down strikes through which workers during the labor movement suddenly reclaimed their own sense of collective power and agency from the factory machines and their owner-operators that had turned them into passive objects, Sartre's description of the emergence of the group coming into fusion provides a social-ontological and intersubjective foundation for the possibility of transformative social change that goes beyond the external categories of much of social theory—for example the category of "class struggle" within the history of Marxist theory itself which could not account for how the revolutionary class would recover its agency as a living social process. And Sartre's new concept prefigured exactly what would take place five to ten years later during the upsurge of the sixties, when human beings (like myself) who had been trapped in the passivity and distance of our socially separated and artificial lives, would emerge into authentic groups in which our essential presence to each other could suddenly become visible, and through which we could generate an extraordinary social energy that could "move" into a movement, ricocheting invisibly but decisively from Berkeley, to Mexico City, to Prague, to the general strike of May '68 in Paris.

The social paralysis of being trapped in and an unwitting agent of the series, and the always potential transformation of the series into the group-in-fusion through which we can overcome our alienation and recover our reciprocal presence to one another as Here and as One (or as "the common individual," in Sartre's terms)—these are very important ideas that Sartre has contributed to establishing the link between the transformation of spirit and the egalitarian and ecological transformation of the material world. But as Gerassi brings out in his interviews, there was something essential that was lacking in these later formulations that was becoming apparent in the world itself in the early 1970s—in the very decay and gradual dissolution of the movements of the sixties that was beginning to take place at the time of the interviews and that is palpable in them.

In one key exchange, Sartre has been describing as a kind of illustrative mini-example of the group-in-fusion a bus ride in which a group of bus passengers who had previously been merely a disconnected series, a line of people waiting for the bus at the bus stop, had transformed themselves into a fused group by persuading the driver to go off his normal route and to drop each of them at their destinations, which in turn leads to the able-bodied passengers taking pleasure in assisting an old woman in a wheelchair to get off the bus and get into her home, and to an overall atmosphere of joy and free conversation erupting into the dead space where there had previously been merely a collection of anonymous strangers. Gerassi responds by saying, in effect, that's all well and good, but those passengers will inevitably go home and the next day they'll be back in line, the weight of historical forces will again overwhelm and condition them, and their hot moment will go cold—just as the sans-culottes of the French revolution returned their power to the elites and lost their transformative energy, just as the Paris Commune had failed to sustain itself, and just as the youth of the sixties were seeing their groups dissolve into internal squabbles or get co-opted by the political parties or become overwhelmed by the legacy of generations of fear of the other more powerful than the momentary unity made possible by the moment of fusion. "To avoid defeat the group-in-fusion must remain in fusion," says Gerassi. "But how? ... If the group-in-fusion is always bound to fail, no matter how much of a residue it leaves around the edges for historians to contemplate, why risk starting it again?"

It is difficult to read these words and not feel that this is exactly the worldwide dilemma of the present moment, that because of the failures of prior social movements and the defeats or distortions of the fused groups that these movements were formed by and inspired, we are unable to risk starting it again and to surrender to the radical hope that this requires of us without a new step in theory to guide and express some new form of social practice. Sartre's own answer to Gerassi is that the process is not circular or hopelessly repetitive, that each such transformative experience is internalized as a historical memory that is passed on, however silently, in the culture and moves the ball forward and furthers the liberatory development of humanity. But even if there is some hope and validity to be found in that response, it seems clear to me that the Sartre of the early 1970s could not yet have grasped that his own thinking was inherently limited by the secular nature of his own conditioning, by his failure to realize that the breakthrough permitted by the fused group can only truly be sustained if it is accompanied by a distinctly spiritual elevation of the heart that requires another and deeper form of communal self-recovery than is conveyed by the idea of the revolution, the rebellion, the instantaneous and sudden rupture of the artifice of the status quo. What is needed is a theory and practice of human connection that has sufficient spiritual depth to gradually heal the fear of the other that has been installed in our hearts by the shocks of our generational and personal conditioning and to elevate the fused group into a beloved community. Sartre helped us by showing that we are always connected even when we imagine we are most separated, and that by turning toward each other in meaningful, life-giving social action we can become the source of each other's completion. When will we have gone far enough beyond his formulations to actually take the next decisive steps toward this redemptive end to "risk starting it again"?

ESSAY SEVENTEEN

PATRIOTISM AT THE BALLPARK

LAST MONTH I DROVE MY TWELVE-YEAR-OLD SON down from San Francisco to Los Angeles to attend Opening Day of the baseball season at Dodger Stadium. We're both Giants fans; we love going to games together; the Giants were kicking off the season against their great rivals, the Dodgers. But it turned out we were going to much more than a baseball game.

Prior to the game, as always, the crowd of some 50,000 was instructed to stand and remove our hats for the Star Spangled Banner. On this ceremonial Opening Day, however, the National Anthem was accompanied by the unfurling of a gigantic American flag that gradually covered the entire outfield. As an opponent of the war in Iraq and coercive patriotism, my son never wants to stand for the Anthem, and I've had to go through verbal contortions to persuade him that in spite of our common feelings about this matter, he should still stand in order to not appear to show contempt for others around us or at least to avoid being punched in the mouth, but that we could do so without standing at attention or putting our hats over our hearts, as is the custom of true believers.

But the giant flag was more morally compromising, and I was the one who snapped when at the height of the ceremony, three Navy jets, described as "bombers" over the public address system, flew overhead with a deafening roar. As I ran up the steps to the rear of the stands to escape with a shred of my conscience remaining, my son shouted "Dad!" and scurried after me not really knowing what panic had suddenly overcome me, the supposedly reasonable, balanced one with all the explanations. And our moral trial wasn't over: the whole thing happened all over again in the "seventh inning stretch" between the top and bottom halves of the inning, when the normal "Take Me Out to the Ballgame" was replaced by a glorious singing of "God Bless America" (since 9/11, this ritual substitution has occurred throughout the major leagues on weekends and on special occasions).

The Giants lost 5-0, but the idea was that at a higher level we had participated in a ritual that had reaffirmed our national unity. The point is the more telling when you consider that since the game was in Los Angeles, and even factoring in the self-selection of those who go to baseball games, more than half that crowd likely voted for Kerry, opposed the war, and felt confusedly pulled along by some iconic larger "We" that overpowered and more-than-half-silenced them.

The point here is that sports as a cultural phenomenon is much more than a game, and also more than a "business" as the media cynics sometimes characterize it—it is an important public activity saturated with moral meaning that plays a role in shaping popular consciousness. And because sports is overlain with this moral dimension, progressives should insist that sports be a contested terrain from a moral standpoint rather than just ceding this cultural arena to the Right as the supposed political haven for winners and tough guys. We have already seen a positive example of this kind of progressive resistance in the worldwide demonstrations against the running of the Olympic torch prior to this summer's 2008 Olympic Games in Beijing, contesting China's claim to international legitimacy as the host of all of the world's sports teams by challenging its occupation of Tibet and its investments in Darfur.

But the same kind of moral struggle should be carried out across the sporting spectrum, including, for example, challenging the willingness of so many American sports teams to require their players to wear the Nike "swoosh" in spite of Nike's exploitation of international child labor, or allowing the noisy louts on Fox Sports Net's "The Best Damn Sports Show Period" to utter any sexist thoughts that come into their minds on national television. If sports are going to be wrapped in the American flag, let's challenge those who do so to also celebrate the positive accomplishments of American social movements and the progressive moral values by which these movements in part have redefined American identity. Major League Baseball's decision to spend the entire 2007 season honoring Jackie Robinson for his courage in risking his life and health to break baseball's color barrier in 1947 is an excellent example of just this kind of public linkage of sport with a commitment to social justice, and it contrasts sharply with baseball's normal fare of military spectacles glorifying how tough we are and how we can kick people's asses.

The moral dimension of sports also plays out in the context of the investment practices of team owners. At the present time, baseball ownership groups and the media who report on them conceive of team ownership as basically a form of private investment like any other, with owners having the right to manage their assets and pursue their own economic self-interest without regard to the moral and social consequences of their actions. But this self-interested and privatized view of the prerogatives of owners and investors overlooks the fact that sports teams have a public and civic relationship with the team's home city, with that city's culture and values, and with the tens of thousands of fans who provide the team with its revenue precisely because of this communal identification. And it's in significant part because of this communal dimension, because teams representing cities travel all around the country to play other teams representing cities (as opposed, say, to conceiving of the games as the Chevron owners vs. the Safeway owners) that baseball has become known as "The National Pastime." This quasi-public nature of the team is what accounts for the fact that Congress has taken upon itself to oversee and regulate baseball in ways that would be inconceivable in the case of most private businesses, recently criticizing both players and owners during televised public hearings regarding steroid use and other drug practices that, according to many members of Congress, undermine the integrity of the "National Pastime" and contradict the morally uplifting influence that baseball is supposed to have on each successive generation. Thus the very same public moral elements of the game that justify the National Anthem, the Navy jets, and other conservative patriotic rituals also provide the basis for an ongoing moral scrutiny by Congress that would be perceived in other corporate contexts as an intrusion on the individual rights of owners and players.

It is now time for the Commissioner of Baseball, in conjunction with the team owners and the players association whose members make such high salaries from the sport, to embrace this public and moral character of baseball and announce that teams will henceforth engage only in socially responsible practices— whether involving investments, employment practices, food service contracts at the ballparks, or really all activities with which the sport as a cultural creation expressive of the whole community are connected. If that kind of transformation in the sport's cultural meaning and identity were to take place, the expressions of patriotism itself would actually mean something human and important linking all of us to the creation of a better world. In an interesting way, that might make the current preoccupation with flags and bombers seem oddly out of place, even shallow.

ESSAY EIGHTEEN

THE PORTRAITS OF
ROBERT BERGMAN

WHEN WE SAY WE SEEK *TIKKUN OLAM*—to heal the world—we implicitly refer to a reservoir of human goodness, a wholeness from which we are alienated and which we call upon each other to restore or even to make manifest in a more complete way for the first time. We don't mean that the world must be fixed, like a fence, but that there is a truth within us as social beings that has become distorted and masked from our own awareness, and yet that can be felt, intuited, and known, and therefore healed from its present fallen state. But to make the case for a *tikkun olam*—to really convince ourselves and one another that this convulsive social healing is possible and is therefore the necessary moral project of our lives—we need decisive reminders that we absolutely do know what we're talking about, that we are referring to something real within and between us that calls upon us to resolve the social illness that separates us and makes us unwell.

The photographic portraits of Robert Bergman—displayed at the National Gallery in Washington, D.C., and on the cover of this book and the pages preceding and following this essay—provide a decisive reminder of this kind. These breathtaking works of art bring us face to face with other human beings. But unlike most face-to-face encounters in which the outsides of two faces are visible to each other from within each viewer's subjective isolation booth, the encounters made possible by Bergman's photos provide sudden moments of the discovery of mutual presence, in which we are pulled out of our customary withdrawn state, the key symptom of our illness, and into a sacred contact with the humanity of the other behind and through the image of the face itself. I call these works breathtaking because they unfailingly cause an interruption or disturbance of my breathing as I experience the shock, and the relief, of being brought into an experience of mutual recognition with one after another of the human beings Bergman portrays—and I believe they will do the same for anyone who contemplates them at full size in the gallery. In each case the trappings of a social identity are there that convey a definite impression of a particular life's circumstances—of one or another legacy of suffering and solitude and also of resilience, determination, and effort—but the accumulation of past influences is in every case transcended by an uncanny illumination, a manifestation of the Holy Spirit that conveys a sense of universal vulnerability and at the same time invincible spiritual strength.

The aesthetic of postmodernism is at odds with the moral conviction inherent in spiritual activism because postmodernism celebrates irony, the glancing blow, a "quotation mark" approach to the social world that is so preoccupied with evading false representations of the self that it participates in the fear of the other that is the source of our problem in the first place. Bergman's art rows mightily in the other direction. Like postmodernism, Bergman takes on the false world masquerading as real, but he does so by making present our inner authenticity and our longing for social redemption through the act of recognition of who we really are. Instead of stranding us in our own isolation through clever facade-puncturing deconstruction, Bergman pulls us straight through the world of appearances and, by making who we really are manifest, shows us in our hearts that healing to become this who-we-really-are is our moral destiny, is what we're supposed to be doing with our lives.

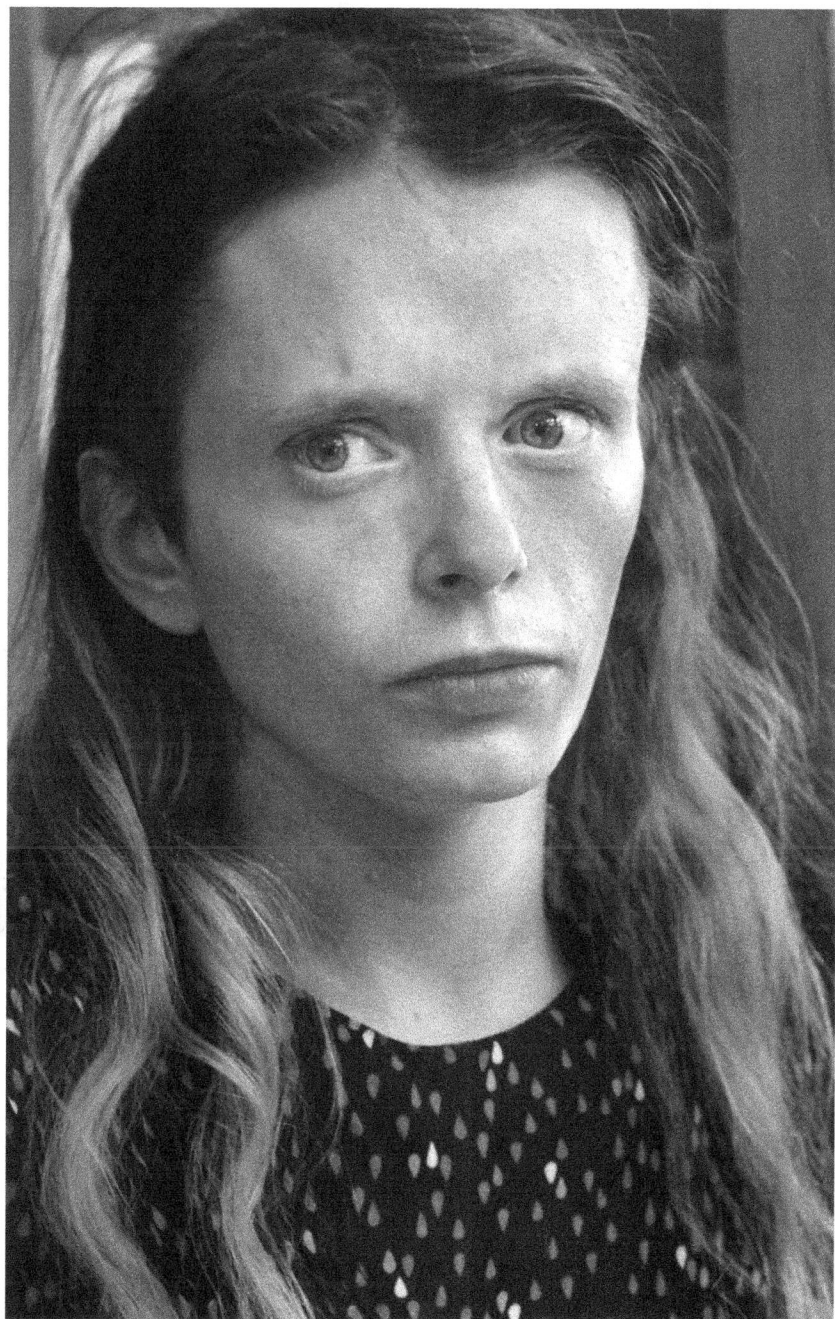

ESSAY NINETEEN

LIVING WITH ILLNESS IN AMERICA

I'M SICK, CHRONICALLY SICK, recovering (I hope) from a long-time prescription drug addiction that I didn't know I had. To even write these words for publication makes me hesitate: Am I facing disgrace by doing so? Will my sense of power in the world or my charisma or sex appeal or worthiness of recognition as still in community be fatally compromised? In saying publicly that I'm sick, I am stating a truth that I am afraid will lead others to feel sorry for me, pity me, subtly withdraw from me, "wonder how I'm doing" but no longer engage with me as a vital participant in their lives, or in life.

This is the secret of living with chronic illness, and it's worse than the illness. It leads us, unnecessarily, to lead two lives: one drawn into the self and preoccupied with the illness and its effects, the other presenting a good face to the "outside world"—faking as much normalcy and strength as possible so as not to face a hemorrhage of identity. Was I strong enough this morning to have been a good father for my seven-year-old son Sam or was I a subtle disappointment? Should I tell him I need to lie down this afternoon and hope so much that he'll just playfully join me, or should I pull it together and play catch in the park like a real father is supposed to do, and put that spring in my step whether it wants to be there or not? If my fatigue or anxiety shows in my speech, will the listeners to my talk be unmoved by my words or otherwise disappointed by my surprising inadequacy? Or can I "summon the strength" to be the me they expect and shut down the voice inside that so resists that summoning of outer power, objecting to my splitting the self that I actually am?

Yet both sides of this split are unnecessary. The preoccupation with inner symptoms results mainly (if you're not facing death or severe pain) from how it may affect carrying forward the outer self to meet and satisfy the expectations of others that you are well. The false lifting-up of the outer self does not reflect a true inability to engage and participate fully in the world but reflects our fear that revealing the effects of the illness will lead others to think that we are not already so engaged.

So instead of teaching with my illness, whose effects are unpredictable from day to day, I cancelled my contract law class for the fall. This would have been completely unnecessary if I could have taught as a sick person, openly revealing the effects of insomnia, anxiety, adrenaline imbalances and other symptoms, instead of feeling I had to teach in spite of being sick and cover the symptoms to the extent that they might arise. I've cancelled talks and avoided other "commitments" because I know or think I know or worry that I can't be accepted in a somewhat weakened or altered state, that I must "rise to the occasion"—meaning pretend that I'm "fine," that I am with everyone in the manner expected of a speaker "like me."

In a larger sense, being sick provides us with a unique window into the price the soul pays for its conditioning. To be well in an artificial society is often to conceal the inner longing for unconditional and authentic love and recognition behind a series of masks that eventually requires forgetting that the mask is a mask, the source of our common emptiness, restlessness, frustration, the silence between us amidst the busyness of our common activities. To engage in *tikkun olam*, to heal the world, transforming our response to sickness might provide an opening to a cure for the functional alienation that so often passes for health.

Instead of having to choose between withdrawing in a kind of shame from the world and covering one's illness to fake being normal, what sick people need is to be fully embraced and included in all aspects of life while being openly sick. This requires the creation of a kind of intermediate space that is socially legitimate, that makes room for the sickness in the manifestation of one's talents and vitality, and that may even bring an element of vulnerability into everyday life that offers a unique contribution to the recovery of our common humanity in undivided form. Ultimately this extends to the collective embrace of aging, dying, and death, our universal destiny, as a sacrament blessed by the full and continuing presence of the other, rather than as the increasingly isolating tragedy that it now usually is, as we each live it out, secretly together, in appearance one by one.

Grant me my real condition, dear Reader, and I'll join you in yours, and all will be well and all manner of thing will be well.

AFTERWORD

THE SPIRITUAL DIMENSION OF SOCIAL JUSTICE

(The Annual Georgetown University Law School Scholarship Lecture to the Georgetown Law School Faculty, April 26, 2012)

WHAT I'M GOING TO TALK ABOUT today is the spiritual dimension of social justice. And in that spirit, let me begin with an eloquent formulation by Martin Luther King: "Justice is love correcting that which revolts against love."

That's one very beautiful way that Dr. King tried to capture the existential grace and recognition and affirmation that comes through the experience of justice and the work of justice in a culture. He also said famously that "the moral arc of the universe is long but it bends toward justice."

Both of these ways of talking about justice begin with the assumption that we are already connected, that we are anchored to each other in our common humanity, and that the work of law and justice is something like the work of a mountain climber, who throws his pick to the top of a mountain, pulls strongly on the rope of conviction that links us to a common vision—our common destination—and then finds his or her steps as a result of that anchorage, in a future vision based on our already existing social bond.

The foundation of that social bond, the basis of it, is what I call the desire for mutual recognition. In our world as it exists, we all spend much of our lives encapsulated in private separate spheres, living out our private destinies in a kind of mutually imposed spiritual prison. But in reality we are always animated by the desire for an authentic mutual connection with another human being, or with many other human beings. Through the experience of mutual recognition, one can sense the other as a Thou, as Martin Buber famously put it in his book *I and Thou* ... we attempt to realize in human interaction the full human presence we are through recognition of the other as he or she really is and through being recognized by the other in precisely this same grounding way. That desire for mutual recognition is a fundamental longing within all human beings that is

171

central to how we act, really at every moment, and any of us who have children know this with clarity, because as soon as children are born, the integrity and authenticity of their animated presence immediately pulls us into their gaze, and one principal joy of having children is rediscovering in ourselves the capacity for that spontaneous sense of being connected to another human being, not mediated by fear or distance.

The problem in our culture is that the desire for mutual recognition is, to a large degree, everywhere denied. It's denied when we pass each other with blank gazes on the street. It's denied when we stare at each other through restaurant glass windows as if we are looking as in a zoo at the person on the other side. And it's denied in the distribution of and internalization of roles that we play within the culture that withdraw us deeply within ourselves and disable us from making manifest the longing that we really are.

When I was in law school in the late 1960s, I used to watch the evening news in Boston. The newscaster's name was Tom Ellis; someone told me he's still doing the news amazingly enough. And every night Tom Ellis would come on and he would say things like "Red Sox Win and a Fire in Rochester, Back in a Moment!" with a glassy-eyed stare, with his gestures just a little bit too far behind. His finger was a little bit late following his hyped-up words, and watching him "perform himself" made me feel very uncomfortable, pushed back into the couch. I felt like I was confronting a persona that was a great mystery to me. I wanted to solve what was going on with this newscaster. What was the nature of his being, how was he manifesting himself? And what I came to see was that he was attempting to enact a role in which he sought to be anonymous by playing a part, and to remove his own authentic presence from the persona that he was playing, in order to "get over on" the activity he was engaged in—to make it as a newscaster. That was a denial of his desire for human recognition, it was a learned condition, a way of manifesting himself in the world that was not actually who he was—a vulnerable, spontaneous, human presence. At the same time, as he was alienating himself from himself—feeling the need to do so based on his history or by the media he was in—at the same time, at a meta level he was transmitting to others, to the viewer, that "this is who I really am." It became impossible to say to him what I'm saying right now, because Tom Ellis was saying simultaneously, "I'm at a distance, I'm playing a role, and this is who I really am." So at the meta level, that doubling of his artificiality and his denial of that artificiality sealed him within himself and manifested that core aspect of playing roles that separates us from each other, and make us unable to see and recognize each other.

Underlying this situation that I'll call mutual distance to the extent that we all, in part, are encapsulated by these roles, is a fear of the other, a fear of being humiliated by the other, a fear that the other will not recognize us in our own authentic or true humanity. And this fear as a chronic existential condition endemic to all of us generates an anxious continual movement from part to part, from role to role, throughout the course of our lives. And because this transmission of fear and denial of our deepest longing to see and be seen by the other moves in a circle—from each of us to the other—across and through the culture, I call the social-spiritual prison that we are in the circle of collective denial. We each internalize the way we experience the world, and unwittingly, we externalize it in ourselves—that alienation or separation from the other—so that we each become inadvertently one of the others to each other, participating in the co-creation of a human universe in which the deepest longings within all of us cannot be manifested, or so we feel.

Having said all that, at the same time, Tom Ellis, the real presence and person, is there. The desire for mutual recognition pulses through him anyway. No one is ever completely robot-ified by these roles that we play. And there is a struggle within the society as a whole at every moment, a co-presence between fear and hope, fear and longing that is always trying to make itself manifest in every two-person interaction, and also in society, politics, and the development of culture. So, that's the human situation as I see it—the human situation in society and in history. This struggle is not all that we are but it's a very important part of shaping the existence of the social universe.

As intractable as this repetitive struggle may seem, there are many occasions when people are able to break on through to the other side, when the power of hope and the realization of our loving and good natures really does overcome the fear, the risk of humiliation and non-recognition. One such occasion is in the generation and manifestation of social movements. I can tell that many of you here have lived through social movements; not all of you, but some of you are certainly old enough to have experienced the upsurge of connectedness that was manifested in the social movements of the 1960s. For you, let me recall the power of the civil rights movement as a redemptive movement of being in which out of the black churches came an upsurge of solidarity of connection and courage that manifested itself in a way that drew many of us into that historical moral and social upheaval. In the process of being drawn toward and then into that movement of being, many of us had the experience of becoming present for the first time, of feeling the vitality of idealism, of being motivated by a moral vision of human good that we could help to bring into being by becoming active participants in and manifestations of it—rather than being more detached, more passive observers withdrawn into ourselves, watching the world as something outside of us. For those of you who have not directly experienced that, I hope you can get a sense of it just from the resonance of my words, as a feeling you yourselves aspire to simply because you are human and because this longing, as I have said, exists within all of us.

Now let me shift to my reason for being here at Georgetown Law School, and the importance of law and legal culture to the forward motion of the movement as a transformative energy. What has happened, and what happens, when a social movement animated by the spiritual force of the longing for mutual recognition and authentic connection enters into the legal arena?

Every movement must enter into the legal arena because the very basis of the movement is to make a claim on the community as a whole for justice. And the social context in which that claim, that moral claim, must express itself is in law, in trying to assert the movement's justice claim in the legal arena. At that moment, the movement for social change faces a significant challenge because the legal arena that we have inherited, and that we live enveloped by, is a legal arena which is de-spiritualized. By this I mean that the framework of American law is based upon the assumptions of what we often call liberal political theory, or the liberal paradigm, a world-view based upon a secular/empirical view of the known universe and an individualistic view of the social compact. But seen from the socially connected framework that I have been articulating, this liberal model or set of assumptions about the world is actually a *social* description of the world in which people are disconnected monads, disconnected from one another—not inherently in relationship to one another as an existential, ontological reality, as I am claiming we truly live it. The longing, the communal longing that I have been emphasizing as inherent in our very being and the desire for mutual recognition expressive of it, is not manifested in our inherited legal paradigm. Like other forms of the denial of the desire for mutual recognition, our inherited legal culture denies this desire by assuming we are ontologically separated individuals whose bond is purely after the fact and voluntary, rather than constitutive of who we are in our very essence before we even become individuals. Important though the liberal paradigm has been historically, in the accomplishments of the 16th, 17th and 18th centuries in establishing the integrity of the individual's freedom of speech, freedom of religion and the protection of the person against the group through the medium of individual rights—as important as this achievement has been, it has now become an expression of the very problem we must overcome if we are to realize our true social nature as inherently loving and generous social beings.

So to reiterate: When I say that our law as it is represents us as disconnected monads, what I mean is that the picture of the world transmitted through law's discourse and processes is one of floating separate spheres, who may come into connection through voting separately to create the government, or through the formation of contracts and a whole variety of other voluntary activities, but who are not inherently already connected in the sense of being constituted by the social bond that I'm trying to describe. The liberal legal world is a representation of the social world that corresponds to and expresses our fear of each other, but masks, obscures, denies our inherent bond and our longing for mutual recognition. Our law institutionalizes, ontologizes, takes-for-granted-as-inevitable the existential separation that we live out painfully in our everyday private existences.

Now we do feel separate. There's a lot of truth to the fact that we do exist as separate beings, and we do have an authentic individuality that liberal political theory correctly recognized and established within historical social thought, freeing the individual in thought from the authoritarianism of pre-existing group life. But when that individuality is severed from the social bond of recognition, the bond of love by which we actually become whole persons, the liberal model conveys to us a sort of entropy of eternal separation: we appear to each other like an unraveling sleeve, like a collection of people constantly moving away from each other, and guarding ourselves against each other, rather than moving into authentic, empowering, recognizing connection with each other.

So the movement when it enters into this "legal world," which is to say when it enters into an imago or collective image of the world that shapes our thinking and our reasoning within law, when the movement must express itself within this framework and discourse, the dimension of our connectedness is hidden, suppressed from the outset in the very world-view embedded in the images and thinking that we have inherited from the project of earlier centuries. Consider, for example, the law of contracts with its emphasis on each transaction as a bargain entered into by two individuals at arms' length, pursuing their respective self-interests. In reality at every moment we as a community are cooperating to co-create the entire socio-economic world through these contracts. In reality the social economy is a vast cooperative encounter; but mediated through law, this cooperative reality is understood as if it were the result of socially separated self-interested activities, bargainers in the marketplace seen as seeking only to realize the benefit of their bargains, rather than to form a cooperative relationship with another in order to bring about a social good. Tort law, to give another example of precisely the same socially separated image that is used to interpret our civil obligations to one another, is mainly about not intruding upon or causing harm to each other's separate existences, about protecting ourselves *from* each other. In the operating room, we have a right not to be harmed by improper medical practice; on the highways, we have a right not to have our cars smashed into recklessly; when we sit down at the dinner table, we have the right not to have the chair pulled out from under us. But this vision of tort law does not describe any positive duty of care, does not call upon any inherent duty to rescue others in distress. There's no civil notion embedded in tort law that affirms our inherent bond with each other, and instead the framework is the socially separated one. The law of property is about the exclusion of people from parcels of land that are demarcated by imaginary lines we institutionalize in the concept of "title," but not about sharing land, sharing the resources of the land together. To cite a well-known example from every first-year course on the subject, consider the law of adverse possession: I've always found it strange that if people inhabit your land for a required legislated period in an open, notorious and hostile way, they get a claim to it, but if they're there out of your generosity, they do not. So no affirmation of a bond occurs because of the shared use of the property, but rather the possessor's rights accrue only out of the antagonistic use of the property. Or finally, consider the way the very same imago is manifested in the law of corporations: In American law, corporations are the creations of socially separated and discrete investors, who don't know each other, and who are not assumed to share the moral vision of the corporation, seeking to invest their money as disconnected monads, as isolated individuals, to maximize their short-term profits. The idea that the corporation would be understood *a priori* as a bond to accomplish a shared social purpose expressive our bond is utterly foreign to the present-day liberal conception, and because of this, the potential social meaning of such a coming-together-for-social good is *a priori* excluded or hidden from view.

When I say that this core image of the socially separated individual, and of society as a mere collection of such individuals, form a kind of collective "imago," what I mean is that legal discourse as a whole transmits what is literally a co-existing imaginary world, internalized by the culture as a whole "alongside" the existential reality of the nexus of human relationships that constitutes the actual world. And as I have said, a central part of the significance of this interpretive, imaginary world, and what gives it its character as "law," is that we understand it to be binding on all of us. That is precisely why every social movement enters the legal arena to do battle in the first place, why it must do so: by appealing to "law," the movement is seeking to make its justice claim binding on the entire community, by having that claim recognized as binding on the entire group. But if you have followed what I have said thus far, if I have made myself clear, you can see what happens when the force of a movement of being founded upon the affirmation of our human connection enters into a universe in which the very experience of social solidarity and connection that's at the heart of what the movement is fighting for, enters into a co-existing imaginary universe that is going to interpret what is taking place, and what is being asked for, through a medium in which people are perceived as inherently separated and as not embodying any inherent spiritual bond. The collectively shared mental image of "society" embedded in our legal discourse *presupposes* that no such inherent spiritual bond exists, that we only become socially connected by virtue of contracts, or legislative democratic action, or in some other way that follows upon our inherent, ontological individual natures. The inherently connected nature of social reality as it really is, with its foundation in the desire for mutual recognition and affirmation, is represented in existing liberal law through an interpretive schema that begins with our inherent separation.

An example of the consequence of this disjunction is reflected in the history of affirmative action, as expressive of on the one hand a movement for social justice, and on the other a legal claim founded upon the Fourteenth Amendment. When the affirmative action remedy emerged from the civil rights movement, it was meant to evoke a moral passion based on our common recognition of the suffering of four hundred years of slavery, of the massive injustice that had been done to the African-American community over that historical time, and this vision of injustice was not just held to by the African-American plaintiffs as discrete persons; it was a vision and a living memory that was expressive of the movement itself as it radiated through the culture. When I say radiated through the culture, I ask you to remember that everything happened all at once during the emergence of the historical movements of the sixties: the civil rights movement, the anti-war movement, the women's movement, the gay and lesbian movement, the environmental movement—they all sprung into being more or less at once, during the same existential flow of time. We know this. Why did they all happen at once? Because there was a breakthrough of empowered connection between human beings—a sense that we could shake the world out of its everyday lethargy and separation and pain and depression, and a common feeling of responsibility and presence to one another accompanied by an idealistic aspiration to create a truly good world. The force of human connection that was released by this upsurge of social being was overwhelming in its connotative, desire-realizing power and its capacity to create change and heightened awareness across the culture as a whole. That's why the Beatles got so much better so fast—I love the early Beatles but I'm saying the remarkable and increasing sophistication of the music that came out of them over time was not just because they were great musicians, but because there was an expressive force in the culture that made this creativity and capacity able to manifest itself at the same time that these social movements were emerging.

Within this milieu of an awakening and heightening of consciousness, affirmative action had a universal appeal because it was redemptive of the suffering of slavery and the injustice of slavery. And here I mean its connotative, metaphorical meaning, not just to African-Americans, but to many, many whites.

When affirmative action first emerged from this awakening life-force generated in significant part by the movement of social being that was the civil rights movement, this connotative, metaphorical meaning of affirmative action was that "we" could all engage—through "affirmative action" in the collective common "affirmative" act of redemption by the act of affirmatively reaching out to people who had been unjustly oppressed over hundreds of years. That was affirmative action's meaning as expressive of the social movement that gave birth to it and that radiated through the culture as a whole.

But when the legalized remedy of affirmative action as a Fourteenth Amendment claim was interpreted through the prism of the socially separated de-spiritualized individuals of the legal universe, it was instantly given a different cast. The spiritual dimension of affirmative action as a resonant, redemptive force that could play a part in "affirmatively" healing the culture of its own injustice was replaced, or better, overshadowed, by a conception in which one person, subject to past discrimination, was asking to have that impediment removed, so that he or she could compete in the marketplace against all of the other individuals on a fair basis. In this latter cognitive schema, expressive not of the movement but of the liberal-legal image-world, you can see that there is no evocation of a pre-existing communal bond that has been ruptured by slavery and its legacy and that must be healed by the affirmative action of the entire group, but rather a conception in which no pre-existing spiritual/communal bond exists, but rather an imposition of "bias" or discrimination among a disconnected collection of abstract individuals. Understood from within this liberal-legal paradigm, it was quite natural for working class whites and others to feel resistant to affirmative action, to feel that if we are living in an individualistic, competitive world in which everyone is pursuing his or her private destiny, they had not done anything to cause this harm to the African-American community so why are they being "singled out" to bear the burden of the remedy of the "past discrimination" of others. In other words, the very conception of an antagonism between competing individual claims within the legal framework presupposed the erasure of the spiritually interconnected meaning that had been generated by the civil rights movement itself as a morally transcendent presence, the presence of the legacy of unjust suffering of the African-American community exerting an ethical call on all of us insofar as we too, inescapably as co-existing social beings, were ourselves part of the interconnection. Once that immanent spiritual bond was presupposed away through the image-world of legal discourse, it was inevitable that the hostility that developed "between individuals" to affirmative action would lead to a loss of consensus in support of it. The issue of affirmative action as a corrective to past discrimination recast the meaning of the impulse toward the healing of historical injustice as a mere equity issue between two ahistorical individual people (or the groups they represented), each with their respective claims in a competitive, privatized, abstract, individualistic universe. So it became, for some, humiliating to advocate for affirmative action or make a claim based upon it because it became a kind of "handout," a stigma of inadequacy, instead of being a source of righteousness, recognition, and healing. It became a source of anger for the excluded plaintiffs alleging "reverse discrimination," who felt that "no one had helped them," that they had not engaged in discriminatory conduct, and that they deserved what they had achieved based on their "better credentials" in the normative competitive universe.

Thus as it entered into and was appropriated by the interpretive schema of legal discourse, affirmative action largely lost its spiritual meaning (although the connotation of that deeper meaning can never be suppressed completely). And a resulting effect of this legalization of the moral appeal to justice is that it causes, to some extent, the movement itself to lose itself. As the movement enters into law and legal culture and then sees itself through the legal mirror provided by the community in response to the justice claim, because the powerful spiritually connecting and redemptive meaning of affirmative action is no longer present, the movement itself comes to define itself in terms of its rights, and in terms of whether it deserves to have more rights vis-à-vis those who are resisting the rights claims. There is an alteration of the existential phenomenological field so that the movement no longer can see itself from within its own generative transparency as a morally transcendent upsurge of social being. And as a result, entry into the legal arena partly undermines the movement's own power; the life-force within it is, so to speak, absorbed into a despiritualized external representation of itself with no immanent historical and concrete bond uniting its members.

So, what do we do about this? How could we change law so that this most "binding" of our cultural institutions could affirm the spiritual dimension of our common existence rather than contribute to obscuring its presence? What could we do to modify, transform, evolve the liberal paradigm so that we can build a vision of, for example, our Constitution that emphasizes the importance of community rather than the importance of protection of the individual against the other, and that emphasizes the other as the source of our completion rather than as a threat that we need to be guarding ourselves against?

The Project for Integrating Spirituality, Law, and Politics is one such effort that I have helped to organize with a number of other lawyers, law teachers, law students and some non-lawyer "spiritual activists." Our project is to try to help build, as part of many other such efforts within legal culture, a way of interpreting and working through social problems as matters of moral justice embedded within an inherently moral universe grounded in our common longing to fully recognize one another's humanity. Our aim is to transform law into the building of a binding culture in public space—in public rooms like courthouses and court-rooms, in written discourses like law books and legislation—that attempts to foster empathy and compassion and human understanding, a force of healing and mutual recognition, rather than the mere parceling out of rights among solitary and adversarial individuals. Among our efforts is participating in and providing support to the development of the Restorative Justice movement, a remarkable attempt to shift the framework of the criminal law away from identifying the crime, finding the wrong-doer, and putting him or her in jail—the traditional model which presupposes that that a crime is the act of a detached individual against the State—to one that fosters direct victim/offender encounters which seek to encourage people who cause harm to address directly the suffering of their victims—to bring intersubjective concreteness to the infliction of human suffering in a way that makes a call upon those who inflict harm to take responsibility for it, to apologize for it and provide restitution, if possible for the harm—and in some circumstances to be forgiven for it and to be reintegrated wherever possible into the community. In its best aspects, restorative justice also incorporates the historical community out of which social harms occur, helps to illuminate the broader origins of the rupture of human connection that leads to the infliction of harm, and at its best helps to heal and transform whole communities as well as those immediately involved in the criminal act itself, the victim and the offender.

I'll tell you one story that reveals how powerful restorative justice can be when contrasted with the liberal model of crime as an abstract and decontextualized individual act. Several years ago in Des Moines, Iowa, two teenagers who identified themselves as skinheads defaced a synagogue with swastikas. They were more-or-less caught in the act, or just after the act, and a creative prosecutor, instead of simply pleading them out or seeking a conviction for vandalism or even prosecuting a hate crime, asked the defense attorney whether the defendants would be willing to meet with the synagogue's rabbi—to seek a new way of responding to an act of this kind that might accomplish more than simply sending these teenagers from their existing unhealthy cultural locations to jail for a short time and back to the same fearful subculture within which they were immersed. The defense attorney and the defendants accepted, even though this meant the defendants' acknowledging their responsibility for what they did, rather than engaging in the more customary liberal, rights-based approach of pleading not guilty, attacking the evidence, and eventually negotiating a plea. It turns out that the synagogue had a number of Holocaust survivors who were still alive, who were members of the synagogue, and who were willing to meet with the offenders to express and to explain the trauma that the swastika triggered in them. So the Holocaust survivors did meet with these two young people, a young man and young woman who dressed and identified as "skinheads," thought they were neo-Nazis, but actually didn't know anything about the Holocaust in reality. From the survivors of the camps, they learned through direct face-to-face encounter the pain of the swastika and the suffering of the camps. This process evidently opened their eyes, not only to what had really happened to the Jews as real human beings, but to the bitterness, pain, and anger in their own lives that had led them to become skinheads in the first place. Following the "victim-offender mediation" as it is called, the young couple acknowledged what they had done and apologized for it. As part of the spiritual plea agreement that resolved the case, the teens performed restitution by cleaning the building, and they studied Jewish history for many hours, learning something of the pogroms and the history of the persecution of the Jewish people. They were apparently transformed by the experience, and as an extraordinary aspect of the overall outcome, the synagogue's rabbi officiated at their wedding.

Not all resolutions of criminal cases by restorative justice processes result in this kind of utopian outcome, but it is very important to see that the very nature of the intervention is based upon a view of violence, of harm, and of healing, and of what constitutes justice that differs sharply from the liberal model which identifies a decontextualized bad act by an individual actor in a despiritualized human universe. Instead of making an intervention by the community that would have sent these two people right back into the same street system that produced them with no change to their spiritual-political selves—the probable outcome of a normal plea bargain or of a conviction followed by a jail sentence—the resolution of this human problem provides an example of how the legal arena can manifest a community response to a harmful event that transforms all the participants, fostering a new kind of mutual recognition of human beings by each other and fostering a depth of empathy, compassion and elevated understanding that is uncommon and not sought in the traditional liberal model. Everyone involved in the Des Moines case took the risk of suspending or setting aside the fear-saturated image-world of the separated and abstract rights-bearing individuals, instead taking the risk of proceeding on the assumption that we are inherently connected beings, bound together by our moral presence in a complex historical set of circumstances—here, the circumstance not only of the Holocaust, but also of the social conditions in our present-day society that produce skinheads. And it is the affirmation of this moral presence inherent in our very social-spiritual make-up that is what makes possible the resolution that was actually achieved, that so to speak points the restorative process in the direction of a new understanding of justice based upon a spiritual and moral resolution that the situation itself immanently requires and calls forth. The story reveals the deep meaning of Martin Luther King's words with which I began this talk, that "Justice is love correcting that which revolts against love."

Our efforts within the Project for Integrating, Spirituality, Law, and Politics are in a series of areas: restorative justice, transformative mediation emphasizing the capacity to foster empathic and cooperative resolutions of civil disputes, the development of remedies that minimize the role that money transfers (or "damages") play in the resolution of conflicts—and maximizing the role that direct human encounters can play in fostering empathy, compassion, human connection and understanding of the factors that have caused these relationships to become broken, to break down. We also aspire to the transform the way law is taught to the next generation of lawyers so that they develop what might be called a "post-liberal" conception of human relationship, and to bring the inherent cooperative force that exists within all of us into the teaching of Contracts, Torts, Property, the Constitution, all legal subjects that are now exclusively taught from the adversarial rights-based point of view. And we're trying to help build new kinds of law practice that incorporate the spiritual dimension of justice into the work of a lawyer, of which perhaps the best example is the Georgia Justice Project, a remarkable Atlanta-based law firm representing poor people in criminal cases from what we consider a "spiritual-political" perspective.

The GJP's office is directly across the street from Martin Luther King's Ebenezer Baptist Church. When the GJP takes on a new client, the two enter into a kind of permanent contract, in which support for the client as a whole person, rather than as the carrier of a mere discrete legal problem, is understood to be at the heart of the representation. The GJP lawyers commit themselves, if the client is convicted, to standing by the client, to visiting him or her throughout the course of his or her prison term, and to providing to the best of the GJP's ability work opportunity and a community for the client after he or she is released, to manifest love and solidarity and concrete help in the rebuilding of his or her life. If the client is acquitted, the client may come and work in local businesses affiliated by agreement with the GJP, in which the client will learn life skills and also experience the validation of his or her essential humanity and worth, helping him or her to overcome the internal feelings of worthlessness or permanent marginality that may have led the client to engage in the activities that got him or her into trouble in the first place. A powerful metaphor for how different the GJP's form of practice is from the conventional liberal firm is that the law office has a kitchen and the lawyers and staff regularly (at least twice a year) hold communal meals for all their current and former clients.

With the Georgia Justice Project as our model, we aspire to help shape for the next generation of lawyers an idea of an open-hearted lawyer capable of seeking a spiritually-informed justice, an integrated person different from the clever manipulator of concepts that we currently hold as an ideal in our law schools—the "arguer" who conforms much more closely to my example earlier in this talk of the newscaster than of one engaged in a calling to help to heal and transform the world, or in the words of our own Constitution to "create a more perfect union."

Through the Project for Integrating Spirituality, Law, and Politics we are trying to show in theory and practice that law and legal culture in its next evolutionary incarnation must begin with the affirmation that the longing for mutual recognition, for social meaning and purpose, and animated by a moral vision of life grounded in our connection to each other as social beings, is what the pursuit of justice requires, because justice itself can only be fully achieved by going beyond the winning of individual rights toward the bringing into existence of the Beloved Community—the incarnation in the present of who we already are in our essence but whom we have not yet been able to make manifest in our social reality.

So, what I'd say as my last word since this is the annual Georgetown Scholarship lecture is that what I believe we now need in legal scholarship is the spiritualization of legal scholarship—by which I mean, that you as writers and legal intellectuals begin with the assumption I have made here that we human beings are all profoundly connected in our social dimension, and that you begin to inform your analysis of legal doctrine and policy with passion that illuminates how we are to make the world consonant with our already existing spiritual-social natures. Legal scholarship needn't be limited to the detached analysis of doctrines and the play of abstract, rational argument; it can rather be a new kind of impassioned interpretation of the very same issues you currently address but that manifests a life-force animated by your own desire to bring about a better, more socially connected, loving and caring world. If as I have claimed today we are already connected, our goal must be to pull us up the mountaintop and not merely wander around the rocks. I think we all would love to read law review articles, more of them, that begin with that moral understanding.

PERMISSIONS

The chapter "Imagine Law" is adapted from the chapter "Law" published in Marianne Williamson's book *Imagine: What America Could Be in the 21st Century* (Rodale Press and Global Renaissance Alliance, 2000), and is reprinted here by permission of Marianne Williamson, editor.

The chapter "Law and Hierarchy" is adapted from the commentary "The Spiritual Foundation of Attachment to Hierarchy" published in Duncan Kennedy's book *Legal Education and the Reproduction of Hierarchy: A Polemic Against the System* (NYU Press, 2004), © by New York University (all rights reserved), and is reprinted here under license with New York University Press.

The chapter "Critical Legal Studies as a Spiritual Practice" is adapted from an essay originally appearing in the *Pepperdine Law Review* (volume 36, Special Issue, 2009), © by the Pepperdine University School of Law, and is reprinted here with their permission.

The chapter "What It Really Means to Say 'Law Is Politics'" is adapted from an essay originally published in this form in the *Brooklyn Law Review* (volume 67, summer 2002), © Peter Gabel, and is reprinted here with the permission of the *Brooklyn Law Review*. An earlier version of the essay was first published in *Tikkun* magazine in 2001.

The remaining chapters are adapted from essays first appearing in *Tikkun* magazine, www.tikkun.org, © *Tikkun*, and are republished by permission of the present publisher, Duke University Press.

Photographic credits are reproduced on the copyright page, with special thanks to Robert Bergman.

ACKNOWLEDGMENTS

Many thanks to Deborah Kory, Julie Pepper Lim, Shanti Prasad, and Alana Yu-lan Price for their excellent edits of earlier drafts, and to Michael McAvoy and Gary Peller for advice and suggestions that greatly strengthened the book.

P.G.

INDEX

activism, social, 110, 113 (*see also* movement, social)

activism, spiritual, 12, 17, 55, 58, 162

addiction, 169

adversarial system, 23, 24

affirmative action, 177-179
    as common recognition of moral injustice, 177
    as despiritualized legal claim, 178-179

alienation, 3, 5, 8, 11, 15, 17, 24, 32-33, 37, 38, 52, 55, 59n22, 117, 119, 126, 147
    "critique of alienation," as related to indeterminacy critique, 51-52
    social, 3, 8-12, 18, 32, 36, 38-39, 41, 53, 71, 114, 117, 120, 148
    spiritual, 23, 29

Andrews, Rhonda Magee, 53, 60n30

Annan, Kofi, 127

apartheid, 25, 65, 125, 126

Arafat, Yasser, 124

authentic connection, 17, 97, 174

authenticity, 3, 22, 33, 95, 97-99, 103, 110, 120, 147, 162, 172

Ayers, William (Bill), 98

Baker, James, 85, 87

Bank Teller, The (Gabel), 1, 10, 13, 14, 59n16, 59n21, 68, 91n17, 109, 114

Barglow, Ray, 137

Being and Nothingness (Sartre), 145, 146

Bergman, Robert, 143, 161-162, 185

Beyt Tikkun, 49

Bill of Rights, 20, 22 (*see also* Equal Protection Clause)

"bittergate," 98

Boies, David, 74, 89

Boxer, Barbara, 106

Brown, Jerry, 106

Buber, Martin, 7, 171

Burger Court, 77, 78, 92n18

Bush v. Gore, 45, 46, 58n4, 58n5, 58n6, 69, 71-91
    and collapse of socialism, 80-83
    and Gore's failure to present moral vision, 84-87, 89-91
    and Reagan Revolution, 75-80
    error of asserting states' rights instead of voting rights, 73-75, 89

Bush v. Palm Beach County, 87

Bush, George W., 71-91, 94, 100, 119

Carter, Jimmy, 127

circle of collective denial, 9

Clinton, Hillary, 83, 97

Clinton, William (Bill), 69, 82-83, 124, 136

Colbert, Stephen, 143

Condemned of Altona, The (Sartre), 147

connectedness, 31, 119, 121, 173-175 (*see also* authentic connection)

connection, authentic (*see* authentic connection)

Constitution, U.S., 14, 20, 22, 57, 74, 77-78, 80, 85, 87-88, 90, 179, 182-183
    as evolving document, 77
    Bill of Rights, 20, 22
    Constitution Article II, Section I, 87, 88, 90
    Equal Protection Clause, 46, 73
    equal protection theory, 90
    (*see also* federalism, new; Original Intent doctrine; states' rights vs. voting rights; Supreme Court, U.S.)

Cook, Anthony, 53

Critical Legal Studies movement, 18, 29, 33-39, 41, 43-44, 46-50-52, 54-58, 59n11
    alienation critique in, 52-53
    indeterminacy critique in, 44-47, 54
    moral and spiritual basis of, 43-44, 52-53
    rejuvenation of, 54-58

"critique of alienation" (*see* alienation, critique of)

"critique of indeterminacy" (*see* indeterminacy critique)

Critique of Dialectical Reason (Sartre), 147, 148

Cultural Revolution, the, 82

culture, 143-170
    and discovery of mutual presence, 161
    role of irony in, 143
    spiritual and moral dimension of, 143-144

Cuomo, Andrew, 106

Darwin, Charles, 14, 114, 135, 136, 139, 140, 141

despiritualized view of evolution, 115, 135

de Beauvoir, Simone, 147

de Chardin, Teilhard, 136

de Quincey, Christian, 140, 59n12

demonization of the Other, 11
    as defense against vulnerability, 11-12
    relation to false group identity, 12

Derrida, Jacques, 47

desire for mutual recognition, 1, 7, 8-10, 14, 17, 18, 22, 30, 38, 49, 51, 56, 61, 64, 68, 97, 107, 113, 118-120, 122, 123, 126, 128, 171-175, 177, 183
    and evolution, 126-129
    and foreign policy, 118-120
    and law, 17-18, 49-52
    and social justice, 171-174
    and United Nations, 121-122, 126-129
    denial of, 7-9, 97-98, 172-174

Devil and the Good Lord, The (Sartre), 147

divided self, 8

Doors, The, 15

Dutschke, Rudi, 32

duty
    of care, 176
    to rescue, 27, 57, 62, 176

Ebenezer Baptist Church, 182

elections, 93-112
    as crystallization of emotional field, 105-107
    as limited view of politics, 67

electoral college, 45, 74, 79, 84, 85, 86, 88

Electric Flag, The, 31

Ellis, Tom, 172, 173

Enlightenment, the, 56, 64

Equal Protection Clause, 46, 73

equal protection theory, 90

evolution, 14, 114-115, 135-136, 139-142
    and limits of scientific method, 139-142
    as upward movement of Being, 141-142
    spiritual element in, 135-136

fear of the Other, 4-6, 22, 28, 44, 51, 58, 61, 68, 100, 103, 114, 119, 127, 146, 150, 162, 173

Federal Reserve, 103

federalism, new, 78, 79, 80, 91n18 (*see also* Constitution, U.S.; states' rights vs. voting rights)

Federalist Society, 29

Flies, The (Sartre), 145

Florida Supreme Court, 71, 73, 74, 87, 88

Forbath, William, 53, 59n29

foreign policy
    and spiritual politics, 117-129
    and "surrounding process," 119-120, 122
    as healing "rotating paranoia," 118-119
    as overcoming cultural humiliation, 118-119

Founding Fathers, 65, 77, 80, 86, 88

Fox News, 106, 110

Frankenthal, Yitzak, 128

Freeman, Alan, 53, 56, 59n24

Freud, Sigmund, 2, 3, 15, 76

Frug, Mary Joe, 53, 59n27

gauche prolétarienne, 148

Georgetown Law School, 171

Georgia Justice Project, 35, 60n35, 182, 183

Gerassi, John, 147, 149-150

Gibson, Charles, 97

Goldwater, Barry, 76

Gorbachev, Mikhail, 127

Gore, Al, 72, 83-86, 113 (*see also Bush v. Gore*)

Green, Art, 135, 136

Harris, Katharine, 75, 84-86

Harris, Paul, 53, 59n26

Harvard Law Review, 29

health care (*see* universal health care)

Heidegger, Martin, 6

Higher Law Symposium, 44, 52

Hussein, Saddam, 119, 122, 127

I and Thou (Buber), 7, 171

imaginary communities
  patriotism and, 10-11
  substitute for mutual recognition, 17

inauthenticity, 3, 147 (*see also* authentic connection)

indeterminacy critique, 36-38, 44-48, 50, 53-55, 57
  relation to "critique of alienation" in
    Critical Legal Studies, 51-52

injustice, social, 6, 63 (*see also* justice)

Integrating Spirituality, Law and Politics, Project
  for (*see* Project for Integrating Spirituality, Law
  and Politics)

Iraq War, 93, 114, 117, 122-123, 126, 127

Johnson, Lyndon, 31, 52

justice
  defined as "love correcting that which
    revolts against love" (King), 19, 24,
    38, 121
  longing for, 20
  social, 22, 34, 52, 77, 100, 142, 154, 171-183
    (*see also* movement, social; social justice)

Kennedy, Anthony, 73, 90

Kennedy, Duncan, 29, 32-33, 35-39, 44, 5, 58n1,
  59n25

Kennedy, John F., 50, 73

Kerry, John, 69, 93-94, 114, 132, 154

Khmer Rouge, 82

King, Jr., Martin Luther, 12, 19-20, 24, 28, 38, 50-
  51, 53, 59n20, 80-81, 84, 87, 89, 143, 171, 182

Klare, Karl, 52-53, 56, 59n23

Korten, David, 26

La Cause du Peuple, 148

Laing, R.D., 8

Lasch, Christopher, 132

law
  and critique of rights, 20-21
  as culture of justice, 17-19
  as denial of spiritual bond, 20-21
  as legitimating ideology, 32
  individualism in, 20-23, 61-63, 174-179
  relation to social movements, 23-24
  spiritual transformation of, 24-28

Law and Economics Movement, 54, 55, 77-78, 80

law school, 28, 29, 32-35, 39, 41, 45, 78, 183
  as training for hierarchy, 32-35, 38-39

legal culture, 17-21, 23-24, 26-28, 47, 48, 52, 55-56,
  61, 63-65, 78, 174, 179, 183

Legal Education and the Reproduction of Hierarchy
  (Kennedy), 29-30, 32, 36-39 (*see also* Kennedy,
  Duncan; law school)

Legal Process School, 54

legal realism, 54

Lennon, John, 28

Lerner, Michael, 12, 110, 121 (*see also Tikkun*
  magazine)

Levinas, Emmanuel, 57, 60n36

liberalism, 5, 6, 15

Los Angeles Dodgers, 153

Madison, James, 80

Mandela, Nelson, 125, 127

Mao Tse Tung (Mao Zedong), 82

markets, 26

Marxism, 4, 5, 8, 13, 15, 54-55, 58, 81, 146-147,
  149

material suffering, 4, 5

materialism, 55, 58, 118, 147

McCain, John, 101

Melancholia, 1-3

Mensch, Betty, 44, 58n3

mindful markets, 26

moral optimism, 12

moral presence, 93-94, 125, 181
  and overcoming fear of the Other, 103
  as manifestation of love and compassion,
    96
  contrasted with "positioning," 93-94
  in art, 161-162
  in foreign policy, 120, 125-126
  in politics, 93-96, 99-101

Mourning and Melancholia (Freud), 2

movement
  abolitionist, 101
  anti colonialism, 68
  antiwar, 43, 68, 75, 177
  civil rights, 23, 30, 43, 50, 67, 75, 82, 133,
    173, 177, 178
  environmental, 50, 55, 68, 177
  gay liberation, 50, 68, 75, 177
  labor, 23, 40, 53, 75, 149
  Occupy Wall Street, 3

social, 18, 21, 23, 36, 43, 46, 48, 49, 51, 54,
  56, 58, 68, 69, 75, 79, 80-81, 100-101,
  106, 109-115, 133, 148, 150, 154, 173-
  174, 176-178
student, 50, 68, 75
women's, 3, 23, 43, 50, 68, 75, 177
workers, 43

mutual recognition (*see* desire for mutual
  recognition)

Murray, Patty, 106

NAFTA, 83

National Gallery, 161

National Lawyers Guild, 33

Nausea (Sartre), 145

Nazism, 10, 11, 19, 44, 181

Network of Spiritual Progressives, 12, 55, 60n31,
  133

New College of California, 39

New Deal, 33, 52, 54, 76, 81, 133

New Earth, A (Tolle), 95

new federalism, 78-79, 80, 91n18

New Right, 14, 54, 58, 68, 86, 92n18, 101

Newsom, Gavin, 131

New Republic, The, 29

New Yorker, The, 29

Nineteen-sixties (1960s), 15, 30-32, 68-69, 173-174
  and Critical Legal Studies movement, 29-34
  and opening up of desire, 30-31
  as "ricochet of recognition," 31, 50-51
  breakthrough of consciousness in, 50-51
  "parallel universe" in, 15

Nixon, Richard, 73

No Exit (Sartre), 145, 146

No Future Without Forgiveness (Tutu), 26, 126

Obama, Barack, 14, 69, 97-98, 99-103, 106-107,
  109, 110, 136

Obama, Michelle, 100

O'Connor, Sandra Day, 73, 90

O'Neal v. Colton School Board, 39-41

Original Intent doctrine, 77, 80

Oslo Accords, 123-126

Other, fear of the (*see* fear of the Other)

Pact of the Withdrawn Selves, 10, 106

"parallel universe," 109-111
  and mutual recognition, 109-111
  as antidote to reciprocal isolation, 107
  in 1960s, 15
  manifested in social movements, 109-111

Parents Circle-Families Forum, the, 128

Paris Commune, 150

patriotism, 97-98, 153-155
  as imaginary community, 10-11
  as substitute connection, 10-11
  expressed through flag pin, 97-98

Peller, Gary, 44, 187

Perkins, Frances, 114

perspectives (*see* ways of seeing)

politics, 10-11, 67-69, 71-91, 97-98, 153-155
  as collective moral presence, 93-98, 101-103
  as merely about elections, 67
  as upward spiritual movement, 68-69

Posner, Richard, 59n11, 78

Post Corporate World, The (Korten), 26

Project for Integrating Spirituality, Law and
  Politics, 39, 179, 182, 183

Rabin, Yitzak, 124

Reagan Revolution, 54, 68, 75-80, 82-83, 91n18

Reagan, Ronald, 14, 29, 46, 51, 54, 68, 69, 75-80,
  82-83

reforms
  educational, 102
  environmental, 102

Reid, Harry, 106

Restorative Justice Movement, 25, 26, 56, 61, 65,
  180, 181, 182

Reverend Jeremiah Wright, 98

Rice, Condoleezza, 100

Robinson, Jackie, 154

Roosevelt, Franklin, 84, 114 (*see also* New Deal)

San Francisco Giants, 153

Sartre, Jean-Paul, 13, 120, 143, 145-151
  Being and Nothingness, 145, 146
  Condemned of Altona, The, 147
  Critique of Dialectical Reason, 147, 148
  Devil and the Good Lord, The, 147
  Flies, The, 145
  Nausea, 145
  No Exit, 145, 146

Scalia, Antonin, 45, 73, 88

Scowcroft, Brent, 100

Security Council, UN, 127, 128

seeing, ways of (*see* ways of seeing)

self-determination, 29, 30, 35, 36, 85

Seuss, Dr., 11, 64

Simpson, O.J., 25

Sixties (*see* Nineteen-sixties)

social justice, 22, 34, 52, 77, 100, 142, 154, 171-183
    defined as "love correcting that which
      revolts against love" (King), 19, 24,
      38, 121
    despiritualized view of in law, 174-179
    social movements and, 173-177
    spiritual dimension of, 171-183

social reality, 1, 9, 15, 32, 48, 113, 120, 177, 183

Social Security, 12, 84, 102, 113-114
    as intergenerational bond, 102
    moral vision and, 114

social theory, 1, 6-7, 149

socialism, 37, 48, 54-55, 80-83

Socratic method, 40 (*see also* law school)

Soviet Union, 46, 76, 81, 146, 148

spiritual community, 47, 57

sports, 153-155

moral dimension of, 154-155

Stalinism, 82

Stanford Law Review, 29

states' rights vs. voting rights, 73-75, 89

Stephanopolous, George, 97

Stevens, Wallace, 93

Supreme Court, Florida (*see* Florida Supreme
    Court)

Supreme Court, U.S., 45, 52-53, 69, 71-92, 102 (*see
    also* Burger Court; *Bush v. Gore*; Warren Court)

"surrounding" process, 119-120, 122

Talking Heads, 141

Texas Law Review, 29

The Butter Battle Book (Seuss), 64

Tikkun magazine, 117, 118, 135, 137, 140

tikkun olam, 111, 118, 161

Tolle, Eckhart, 95

Tribe, Laurence, 74, 89

Truth and Reconciliation Commission, 25-26, 123,
    125-127

Tushnet, Mark, 44

Tutu, Desmond, 25, 26, 125, 126

Two and a Half Men, 143

United Nations, 5, 121-122, 127-128
    as manifestation of desire for mutual
      recognition, 121-122, 126-129
    contrasted with nation-states, 122

United States Supreme Court (*see* Burger Court;
    Supreme Court, U.S.; Warren Court)

Unity of All Being, 121

universal health care, 12, 57, 82, 95, 133

victim-offender mediation, 181

Viet Cong, 52

Vietnam Veterans Against The War, 94

Vietnam War, 30, 32, 50, 52

Von Trier, Lars, 1-2

voting rights, states' rights vs. (*see* states' rights vs.
    voting rights)

ways of seeing
    Freudian, 1-4
    Liberal, 5-6
    Marxian, 4-5
    scientific, 139-142
    Spiritual-Political, 6-13

Warren Court, 77

Whitman, Walt, 75, 85

Wright, Jr., Jeremiah A., 98

ABOUT THE AUTHOR

PETER GABEL is former president of New College of California and was for thirty years a law professor at New College's public-interest law school. He is Editor-at-Large of *Tikkun* magazine, a co-founder of the Critical Legal Studies movement in legal scholarship, and the author of many articles on law, politics, and social change. He lives with his partner Lisa Jaicks, a union organizer with Unite Here, and their son Sam, in San Francisco, and he is president of the Arlene Francis Center for Spirit, Art, and Politics in Santa Rosa, California. His last book was *The Bank Teller and Other Essays on the Politics of Meaning.*

qp

Visit us at *www.quidprobooks.com*.

www.ingramcontent.com/pod-product-compliance
Lightning Source LLC
Chambersburg PA
CBHW070912270326
41927CB00011B/2546